Growing Roots

Italians and Croatians in the Development of the Western Australian Timber Industry

Christina Gillgren

SALINA BOOKS

© Christina Gillgren, 2024

This book is copyright. Apart from any fair dealing for the purpose of private study, research, criticism or review, as permitted under the Copyright Act, no part may be reproduced without the permission of the copyright owner.

ISBN-13: 978 0 6485429 6 4
ISBN-10: 0 6485429 6 4

Front and back cover design and graphics, Bjorn Gillgren
Front cover photograph courtesy of Joe Palandri
Page Layout and Typesetting by Bjorn Gillgren

Printed by Ingram Spark

Published by Salina Books, Perth, Western Australia

Copies of this book may be obtained from most online book stores. Alternatively send email to: salinabooks@gmail.com

Fifty four oral interviews covering the period from 1919 to 1969 were conducted for this book. All interviewees gave their consent for their names and experiences to be published. The interviews and accompanying transcripts are held at the Battye Library of Western Australian History in Perth.

Dedicated to the women and men
in this book

'The eyes of others are the mirrors in which we learn our identities.'

Hegel

Contents

Acknowledgements i
Introduction 1
1 'White-anting the British Stock' 5
2 'Axes Swung by Aliens' 31
3 Survival: Naturalisation and Mobility...53
4 Aliens of all types: Civil, Friendly and Enemy Aliens 77
5 Italy surrenders: ex-Internees and Prisoners-of-War 93
6 Desirable Types..117
7 Carving Up the Forest Logging Reserves 143
8 Post-war Migration and Competing Interests 165
9 Growing Roots 181
Oral Interviews 207
Bibliography 211
About the Author..217
Addendum...219

Acknowledgements

Telling the stories of the over fifty Italian and Croatian immigrants who came to work in Western Australia's south-west timber industry in the previous century has been a long-held goal. Yet when confronted with the mammoth task ahead my first attempt was short-lived.

I am therefore especially grateful to the persistence and persuasiveness of two people who showed great interest in my project: Nicky Hodgson who persuaded me to re-start the journey of disentangling their stories from my previous academic work and Sue Siddall who encouraged me to keep on going through the first stumbling blocks.

I am indebted to my readers, Dr Colleen Liston (Busselton Oral History Group), Nicky Hodgson, Sue Siddall and Chrissy Fletcher for taking the time and trouble to read the final draft of my work, and for their useful comments and encouragement. Notwithstanding this, the responsibility for any errors or omissions remains my own.

I am truly grateful for the generosity of the fifty or so men and women I interviewed in welcoming me so warmheartedly into their homes and for the trust and faith which they placed in me in sharing their life stories, documents and photographs. It gives me great pleasure to have finally honoured a commitment to them to have their stories told in the public domain.

Finally, to my husband Bjorn who took on the painstaking challenge of converting thirty-year-old computer files, photos, graphs in readiness for the publication, the word 'thanks' seems totally inadequate.

Maps iii

Map 1: State Forest Areas in Western Australia's South-West to 1925

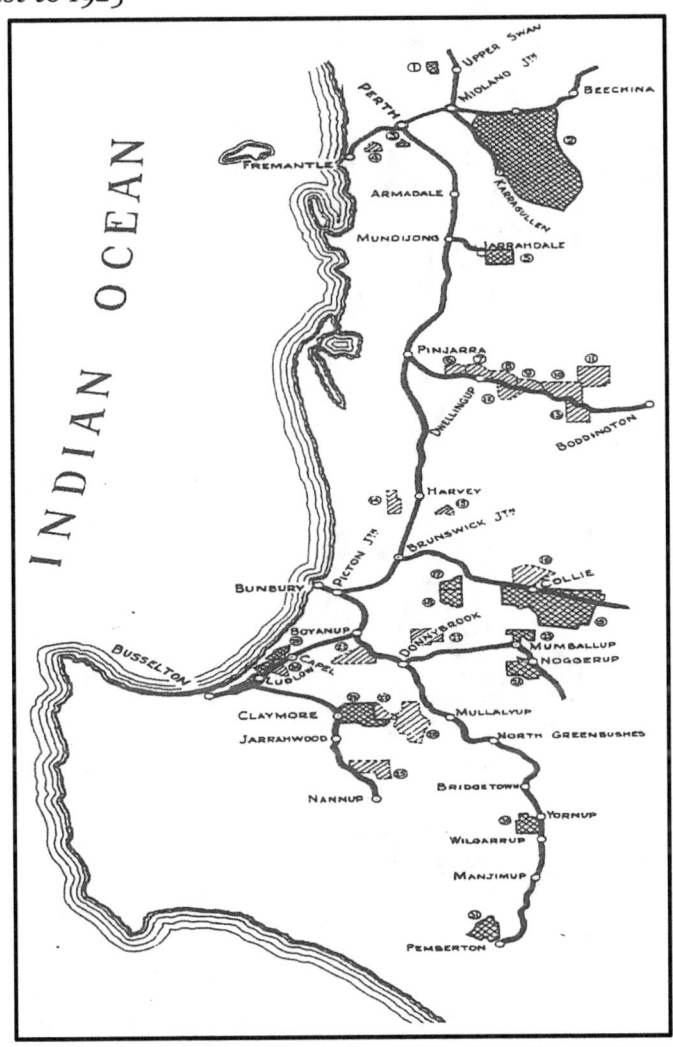

NB: The unshaded areas, and especially along the south-west coastal region, contained large reserves of timber which were privately owned, and therefore not subject to Forests Department control. The shaded areas refer to the stages of management and utilisation of timber under the Working Plans for each area. (Forests Department Annual Report 1925)

Map 2: Extent of State Forest to 1924 (black shaded area) and to 1930 (grey shaded area)

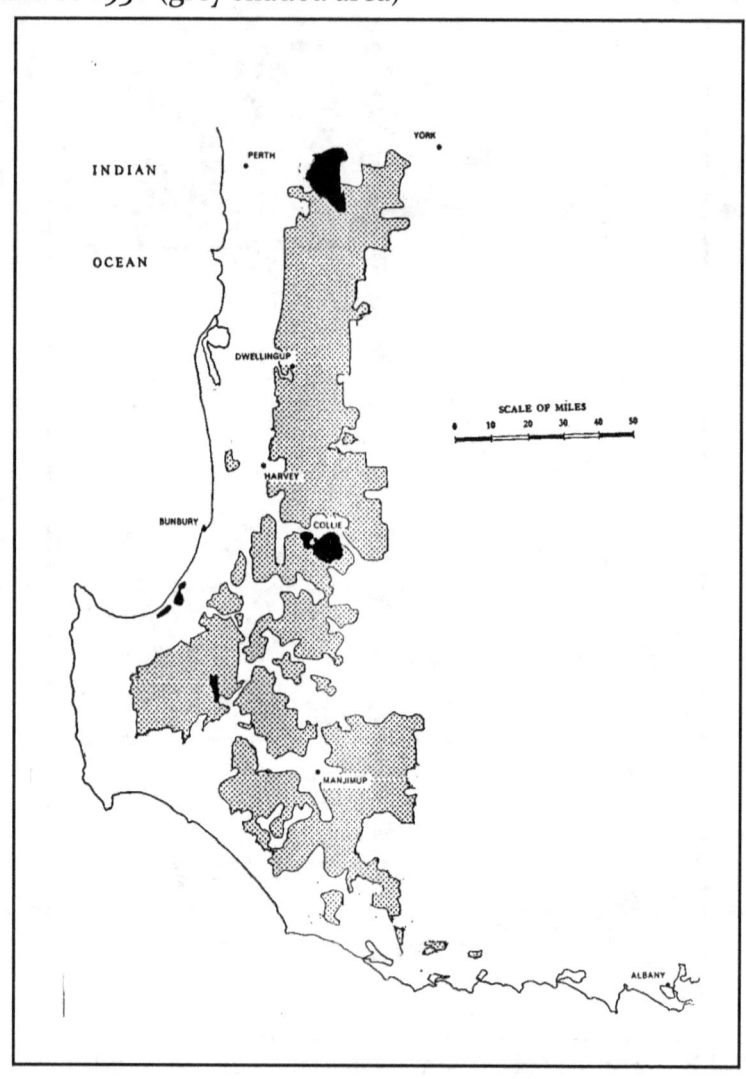

Western Australian Forests Department, 1969

Maps

Map 3: Forest Zones and Pine Plantations in Western Australia in 1956

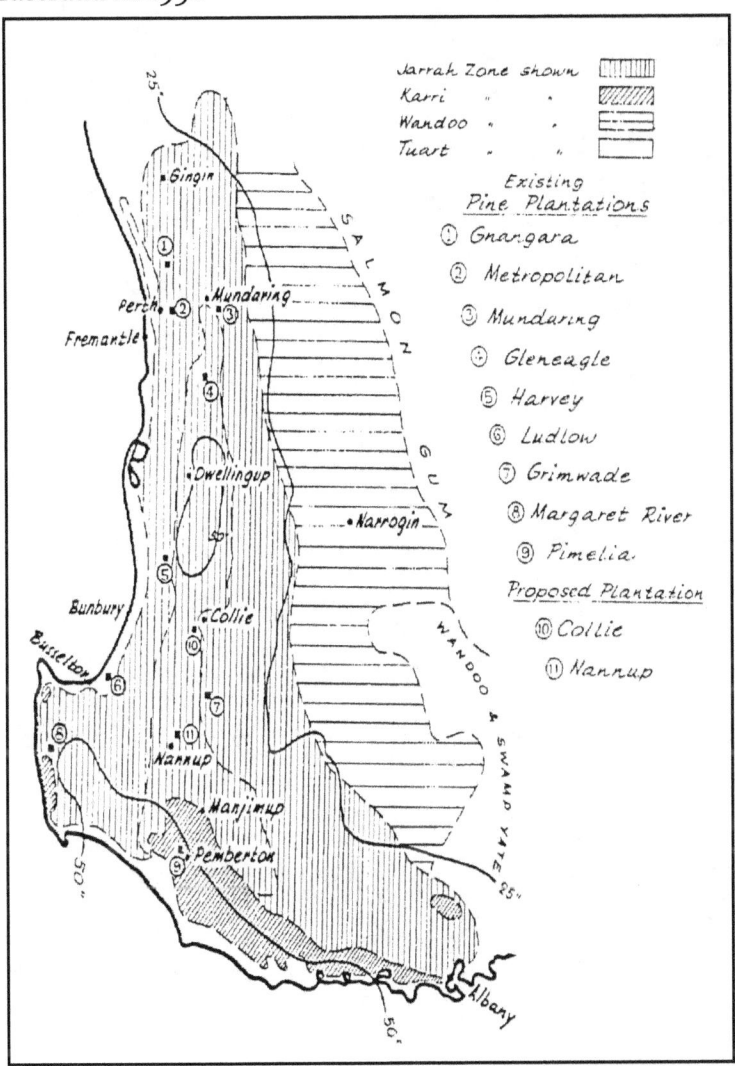

Forests Departments Annual Report 1956

Introduction

When Australia became a nation in 1901, the newly formed federated government, while very keen to have settlers, was predominantly concerned with preserving Australia for its 'white' citizens. In the first decades of the century, the arrival of increasing numbers of southern Europeans fuelled concerns that their influx could undermine the predominantly British character of the Australian population. Xenophobic sentiments targeted Southern European groups who were considered inferior and therefore 'less desirable'.

In Western Australia, the first substantial numbers of Italian and Croatian workers arrived in the early to mid-1920s. As their numbers increased significantly in the latter half of the decade, they were met with opposition, antagonism and restrictions.

The industries which offered work opportunities included the goldfields, the wood lines and the timber industry. These rural industries provided unattractive, harsh and often dangerous work and low pay. This book focuses on those Italians and Croatians who moved into the south-west timber industry where work was more readily available. However, the vastly diminishing forests resources had by this stage become a huge cause for concern. A Forests Department was established in 1918 to act in the interest of conservation and dedication of forests. It was not long before Italian and Croatian timber workers found themselves caught up in the ensuing conflict between the preservation of forest area and the alienation (release) of forest land for agricultural settlement - a conflict that raged for most of the interwar and early post-war period.

This book is based on extensive interviews with over 50 immigrants who worked in the south-west timber industry to around 1970. It tells their stories, including their families, lives and experiences. The book also explores their contributions to the development of the south-west of Western Australia, and particularly to the timber industry and in the clearing of land. This was an industry which accommodated numerous Italian, Croatian and other European migrant workers over this time.

The Timber Industry

The timber corridor in the south-west of Western Australia extends inland from Geraldton and includes the south-west land division to Albany and eastwards as far as the goldfields. For this book, the timber industry has been limited to the timber corridor south of the Perth metropolitan area and excluding the goldfields.

Establishment of a Forests Department

Before the passing of the *Forests Act* of 1918, the vast forest resources of the State had been, to all intents and purposes, at the disposal of any who cared to make use of them. With no restrictions on cutting and no attempts to reforest cut-out areas, the future of the forests had looked bleak. The acting Conservator of Forests had written in his report in 1917 that:

Introduction

> Forests, instead of being regarded as assets, were looked upon as irritating excrescences to be sawn, ring-barked or otherwise destroyed to make room for the settler.

As a result, by 1920, out of the original 8,000,000 acres of prime jarrah country, not more than 2,000,000 acres remained.

In its attempts to preserve forests, the Forests Department focused its attentions on controlling the hewing of timber especially on private land. Hewing consisted of cutting timber by hand to shorter lengths, mostly to produce railway sleepers. Its greatest concern was the lack of control over 'sleeper hewers who were running over the country and picking only the best timber' - a practice that was encouraged to support a lucrative export trade in railway sleepers. Unfortunately hewing was one of the main activities that provided work opportunities to Italians and Croatians. A frustrated Forests Department exploited resentment to the presence of these migrant groups in the timber industry to achieve forestry control. In doing so, it fostered ethnic stereotypes and reinforced their inferior status. This situation underpinned migrant work experiences in the timber industry.

Terminology

The term 'Yugoslav' used to include the southern group of Slavic peoples which include Croatians and Dalmatians is offensive to many members of these groups, and so this term has been restricted to archival records. After having consulted those interviewed, I have adopted the term 'Croatian' as an identifier for these groups.

Another problematic category widely used in official sources and Forests Department records is the term 'southern European'. However because of negative connotations associated with this term, I have referred to Italians and Croatians by their ethnicity wherever possible.

Interviews

Fifty four oral interviews covering the period from 1919 to 1969 were conducted for this book. The interviews and accompanying transcripts are held at the Battye Library of Western Australian History in Perth. All interviewees gave their consent for their names and experiences to be published.

1

'White-anting the British Stock'

The increasing numbers of southern Europeans arriving in Western Australia from the 1920s caused considerable agitation in the press and in parliament for measures to limit their entry. Growing antagonism to their presence was given free rein in the local press. An article in the *Daily News* in December 1924 headed 'Influx of Southern Europeans: A serious position', stated that 1874 foreigners from southern European countries had landed in Fremantle during the year and had found work upon arrival. The article lamented that at the same time a greater number of Australian-born than was usual for the time of the year were unemployed.

Immigration legislation

Immigration laws defined who was eligible to migrate to Australia, and hence who was excluded, and naturalization laws constrained the rights, work and movement of aliens who had been allowed entry into Australia.

In 1920, the national parliament introduced three pieces of legislation: The *Immigration Act Amendment*, the *Nationality Act* and the *Aliens Registration Act*. These Acts tightened entry controls and increased restrictions to non-British migrants (aliens) already in Australia. They extended the period of residence from two to five years before an application for naturalisation could be granted and requiring aliens to register their whereabouts and inform authorities if they changed their place of abode.

A Treaty of Commerce between Great Britain and Italy dating back to 1883 placed Italians in a special position to travel to Australia at liberty. However from 1921 immigration officials adopted a quota system and a landing-money requirement to deter southern European immigrants. Quotas were fixed limits that applied within a given time frame and were used to restrict entry (or exit) based on criteria such as nationality, occupation and class. The landing money requirement, on the other hand, was far more rigidly applied. Despite these restrictions, Italian immigrants to Western Australia more than doubled between 1923 and 1924 from 328 to 1,059 arrivals. It was a similar situation for 'Yugoslav' arrivals. Census figures show that there were 524 residents in Western Australia in 1921 and this number increased to 2,322 by 1933.

Widespread unease within the Australian community placed the federal government under great pressure to regulate to restrict the immigration of those Europeans now referred to as 'white aliens'. Questions were raised in the Western Australian Legislative Assembly regarding the regular arrival of a large number of 'foreign immigrants' many of whom were said to be stranded in the city, sleeping in empty houses and without means of obtaining food. In response to public pressure, the Federal Government passed an Amendment to the

Immigration Act in 1924 which further restricted entry to those who could afford to meet the landing-money requirement and survive economically until work was found.

Despite the concerns expressed about alien migration, in most years there was not enough interest to fill the quotas.

The Timber Industry

Prior to the First World War, Western Australian timber had accounted for almost 10% of the state's total exports, making it second in importance to gold as an export revenue earner. The outbreak of war in 1914 brought an abrupt end to the tremendous growth in the timber industry.

Before the passing of the *Forests Act* of 1918, there were more than 2,000 men employed in the timber industry. By 1922 the number had fallen to around 1,600, and throughout the interwar period the numbers fluctuated greatly between around 1,000 and 2,500, often with the greatest variation being recorded over a period of months. The main sectors of the timber industry were sawmilling and hewing, with jarrah as the primary timber. Hewing was a major source of timber production, at times accounting for up to half of the total quantity of timber produced and, occasionally, more than half of the number of timber workers.

Over the interwar period, the timber industry was one of boom and bust and the number of sawmills fluctuated greatly according to its fortunes. With the advent of a mild boom in 1922 the number of sawmills increased from 23 in 1917 to 114. The mills were concentrated in eight areas: Albany, Bridgetown, Collie, Donnybrook, Jarrahwood, Manjimup, Mundaring and Pinjarra. Apart from a short-lived boom in the mid-twenties, timber lost ground as a revenue earner as timber exports fell to under 3% of the total value of exports in 1934, recovering slightly to about 5% by 1938.

In times of downturn in the industry, the presence of Italians and Croatians particularly in timber hewing on private property attracted strong protest. Their unpopularity provided an opportunity for a newly established and determined Forests Department to fulfil its charter of establishing its control over all areas of forest, particularly on private property. The department's opposition to the felling of trees, especially with the lack of regulation on private property, was transformed into a battle against southern European timber cutters. This paved the way for increasing restriction of work opportunities for these timber workers in the 1920s.

Forests Department

Following the *Forests Act* of 1918 and the creation of the position of Minister for Forests, a Forests Department was established. The Department had full control of forestry matters including regulation of timber workers as they related to Crown land.

Private property alienated before the passing of the *Forests Act* included vast areas of forest land and was a major source of hewn sleepers. However the Forests Department had no control over the hewing of timber or to registration as a timber worker on private property. The Department's view by 1919 was that the *Act* had legalised the destructive sleeper hewing industry which had ruined much valuable timber. It deplored the 'prostitution of one of the finest of the world's hardwoods for such a use'. The Department sought greater restriction in this area so that a sustained yield could be assured (Refer Map 1).

The Forests Department's objection to hewing, especially on private property, brought it into direct confrontation with those who supported land settlement schemes. To a government and a public committed to encouraging immigration and increasing the population base of Australia, the Forests Department's policy and duty to conserve the forest was unpopular. Public debate was divided over competing demands: on the one hand, of forest preservation and conservation and, on the other, of land settlement.

Land settlement schemes

Land settlement schemes were seen by the Commonwealth Government as an important part of Australia's immigration and population policy. It wanted to boost population numbers in the face of an ever-declining birth rate. Western Australia put forward the first and largest of the state schemes that envisaged bringing at least 25,000 men, women and children to the State each year.

Although the 1920's premiers' conference had made a commitment to the dedication of state forests, James Mitchell, Premier of Western Australia, was apprehensive of what he considered to be the 'extraordinarily extensive powers' granted under the *Forests Act* to the Conservator of Forests over land dedicated as State forest. The Premier commented that the Conservator of Forests had 'a profound desire to protect practically every tree growing in Western Australia'. He feared that this would hamper the government's land settlement policy.

The Forests Department answered public criticism of forestry conservation policy by pointing out that the original 8,000,000 acres of prime jarrah country had been decimated with only a quarter of that amount of jarrah forest left. It claimed that approximately fifty thousand acres of karri forests had been destroyed in an almost criminally wasteful manner. The Department condemned:

> the callous and expensive destruction of so many magnificent trees caused by Group Settlement. ...Complete clearing was abandoned and it became the custom to ring the big trees and leave them to die.

Italians and Croatians: work opportunities

Western Australian statutes stipulated that no work restrictions applied to aliens except for entry into the public service. Aliens could register as timber workers, but registration was not necessary for those operating on private property. In practice, however, it was a different story. In the case of sandalwood cutting, for example, sandalwood licensees could only employ natural born or naturalised British subjects, despite there being no legislative impediment for aliens such as Italians and Croatians.

Many Anglo-Australian registered hewers were loath to move away from their families to areas such as Margaret River where the Forests Department was willing to alienate land for settlement. This left the door open for new arrivals in search of work. As the numbers of Italians and Croatians in the timber industry and particularly in sleeper hewing grew, their presence attracted attention especially in recessionary periods. It was their misfortune that the activity that offered the best work prospect was one to which the Forests Department was strongly opposed.

Italians and Croatians in the south west timber industry

Croatians such as Cvitko Ucich and Italians such as Giacomo Palandri had worked in the timber industry in the first decades of this century. Ucich, a Dalmatian Croatian, had arrived in Western Australia in 1914 and had had to register as an enemy alien. However, it was not until the mid-1920s that substantial numbers of southern European workers moved into the south-west timber industry. Italian and Croatian immigrants took work wherever it was available and provided a clearing and hewing workforce wherever the need for their labour arose.

In December 1922, a number of Italians arrived unexpectedly in Western Australia. The *West Australian* newspaper reported that the New Settlers' League previously accustomed to dealing with 'immigrants of our own blood ...rose to the occasion' and found jobs for them on clearing projects. The League stated that they did work which:

> had earlier been refused in disgust by a British immigrant who told Premier Mitchell that it was 'black man's work' and he wasn't going to do it.

Details of migrant workers in the timber industry in the early 1920s are sketchy and the first clear indication in Forests Department records of the presence of a 'Southern European' workforce in timber hewing emerged in 1925 when A Forests Department Report for jarrah forests mentioned that 23 Italians were engaged in cutting a large quantity of sleepers on private property at Noggerup.

Nomination and sponsorship schemes

Many of the men who came to Australia in the interwar period such as Basileo Dell'Agostino and Giuseppe Palandri were sponsored by their fathers, some of whom had been travelling to Australia since before the turn of the century. Pietro Baruffi arrived with a friend, Joe Betti, who was returning to work in Western Australia after a number of years in Italy. Luigi Bertelli was sponsored in 1934 by his father who, in turn, had been sponsored in 1927 by his brother, Giovanni Bertelli, who arrived in 1909 after jumping ship in Fremantle.

Giacomo Palandri and Basileo Dell'Agostino arrived in 1925 under the £10 landing money restriction. The following year, Dell'Agostino and his father nominated Basileo's mother and brother. Both Mate Alac and Stipe Viskovich arrived in 1926 under the £40 landing money requirement.

Mirroring the experiences of many who migrated during this period, Mate Alac had to borrow money from his father to meet the costs. Stipe Viskovich's father was in New Zealand, his whereabouts unknown, and Stipe had come out to Australia on his own. On the ship travelling to Australia, Stipe met Clem Sumich who was coming to join his brothers hewing on private property in Boddington, and Stipe was invited to go along with them. He went on to sponsor his brother Klem Viskovich in 1927.

Stipe Viskovich, at the time of interview in 1995 living in retirement at Millenden in the Swan Valley, stated that one could:

> go on sleeper cutting any time ...that's a job nobody wants but a migrant.

This view was supported by Vince Nani, and Pietro Baruffi. Similarly, Albert Piacentini recalled at his home in Glen Iris that in the interwar years, his father worked as a sleeper cutter because it was 'the only industry'.

Ivan Surina, a hermit in his nineties who, in 1995, still resided at the Donnelly River Mill site, succinctly summed up the feelings of many:

> you got conditions, you have to get good pocket. If it don't suit you, you can go back straight away. Forty sterling in those days, eh!

Many new arrivals joined relatives and friends at their work sites. This contributed inadvertently to the concentration of members of an ethnic group in one location, one such example being the hewing team at Roelands. Some of the earlier immigrants depended on work being readily available after arrival for survival. Pietro Baruffi, for example, arrived in Western Australia in 1921. Baruffi's father had given him some information about the availability of work in Western Australia. He arrived in Fremantle in 1921 to work in the timber industry with £2 in his pocket, 'just enough to buy his broad-axe and wedges and whatever tools they used'.

Language

Language was also a factor in determining where the Italians and Croatians found employment and it influenced ethnic group settlement. Stipe Viskovich found it difficult to learn English and this restricted his choice of work to hewing with a group of fellow Croatians. In the case of Ivan Kusurin, he teamed up with Mate Alac who he told me 'could get by' in English as he couldn't speak the language.

Figure 1.1: Bertelli Sponsorship Chart

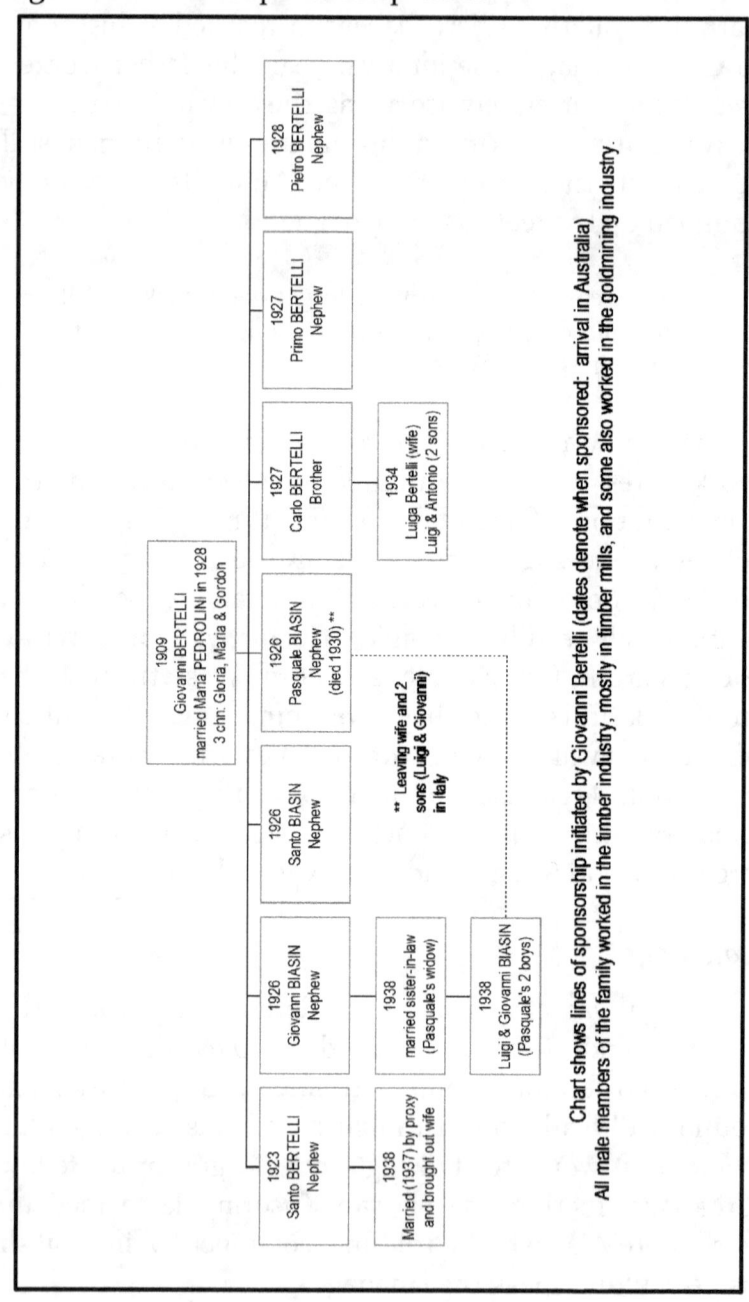

Conditions were tough for some Italians and Croatians from the moment of arriving in Fremantle, when the people who sponsored them failed to meet them. Luigi Bertelli related how migrants were often left stranded by those they were counting upon to help them with the language, find their way around and find work in the first difficult few weeks after arrival.

Living conditions

Letters of complaint and petitions to the Western Australian Premier levelled various accusations at Italians and Croatians, a consistent theme being that:

> these timber workers were used to the lowest standard of living in the civilised world.

However, many immigrants were startled by what they saw as the lack of development in Western Australia. Basileo Dell'Agostino, aged 87 when he was interviewed at the Ocean Star Hostel for the Elderly in Bunbury, recalled that when he arrived in Fremantle in 1925, he was shocked by the state of all the buildings which seemed to him to be no more than 'shacks'. He recounted his disbelief when his father showed him around Nannup, where he started hewing, stating that the village was 'two, three shaggy houses, that's all'.

Almost all of the Italians and Croatians I interviewed started off in the bush as unregistered hewers, cutting sleepers on private property for sub-contractors, constrained by the unavailability of other work. Many were unprepared for the harsh living and work conditions that this occupation imposed upon them. Luigi Bertelli and Basileo Dell'Agostino were respectively 15 and 16 years old when they started cutting sleepers.

Peter Ucich, Vince Nani and Mate Alac were 18 years of age. Andrija Vlahov arrived in Western Australia in 1926 aged 16 to join his father cutting sleepers on private property in Greenbushes. On his first day he was handed a broad-axe with instructions to start logging with his father. He recalled 'going behind the trees and crying - where no one could see him'.

In his autobiography *Into The World*, Mate Alac described the harsh world that confronted him upon arrival in Western Australia in October 1926 when he went straight to cut sleepers on private property in Harvey for the Urlic brothers:

> There were fifteen cutters at this camp. Mate and I made a tent and Stric Jure showed us how to make a bed. We put four posts into the ground. Each one was forked on the top. We then put two sticks through a chaff bag which served as a mattress and attached it to the four posts. Uncle said 'This is your bed - if you can't sleep alongside each other then sleep head to tail'. That is how we slept; imagine how we kicked each other in the chin all night.

Stipe Viskovich described how working in the hewing industry meant sleeping 'out in the moon'. After arrival in Fremantle in 1926, he went to work for sub-contractors cutting timber in Boddington and later in Roelands:

> When you are on a camp, you live, more or less ...in primitive, like Aborigines. You haven't got any facilities, you haven't got any toilet, you haven't got any showers ...you have got warm water in a kerosene tin to have a bath. That's how we living ...food, you get it from a town, bring it once a week.

Ivan Surina camped in a hessian tent in the Tullis area where he was cutting sleepers on his own. The only other human he saw was once a week when food was brought out to him.

Timber hewing

In the 1920s, hewn timber production accounted for roughly a quarter of the total amount of timber produced and peaked in 1927 (Figure1.2). Whereas hewing was carried out on both Crown land and private property, most of the increase in hewn timber came from private property where Italians and Croatians predominated (Figure1.3). There was a slight drop in the number of registered hewers from 1925 as compared with the small increase in hewn timber production on Crown land. This fall can be explained by the emergence of group hewing permits coupled with a shift in the ethnic composition of the workforce as Italians and Croatians joined the hewing industry, working on private property and therefore invisible in records of the numbers of hewers.

The beginnings of group hewing permits are not clear. Mate Alac mentions them in his interview and they appear in many Forests Department records from around 1927. For instance, the 1927 hewing permit entries for one of the permit holders, T. D. Bonola, showed this as a 'group-hewing permit'. Whilst only registered hewers could be employed under these permits, hewing was often casual work and group hewing provided greater continuity of work for hewers. It is presumed that this accounted for the increase in production despite the decrease in the number of registered hewers.

Figure 1.2: Hewn Timber production in relation to total production and number of registered hewers

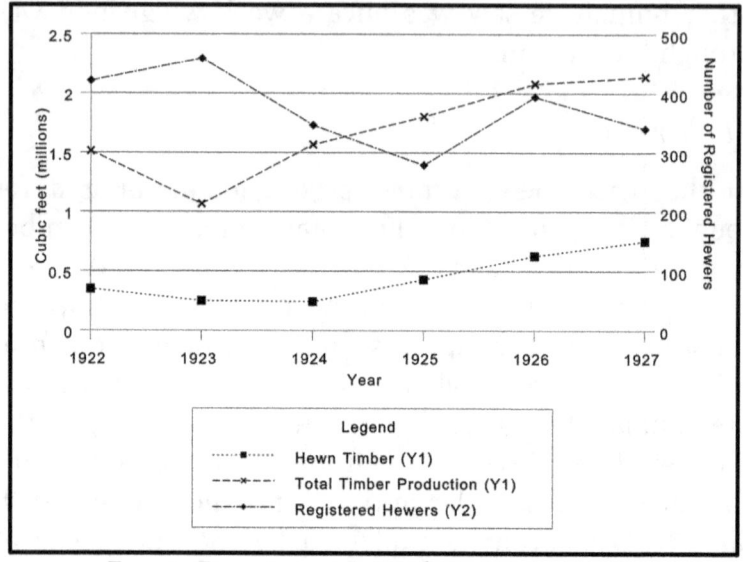

Forests Department Annual Reports 1922-1927

From the mid-1920s, the Forests Department had been moving to restrict hewing permits on Crown land. The Department tried, to no avail, to curtail hewing on private property and appeals to regard forests as an asset to be managed had fallen on deaf ears. However, the entry and concentration of southern Europeans into the hewing industry provided an opportunity which the Department perceptively exploited. By focusing on the ethnic composition of the hewing workforce and exploiting adverse public sentiment to their presence, it now had a pretext that could be used to achieve its objectives of controlling all hewing operations.

Figure 1.3: Hewn timber production on private property and Crown Land

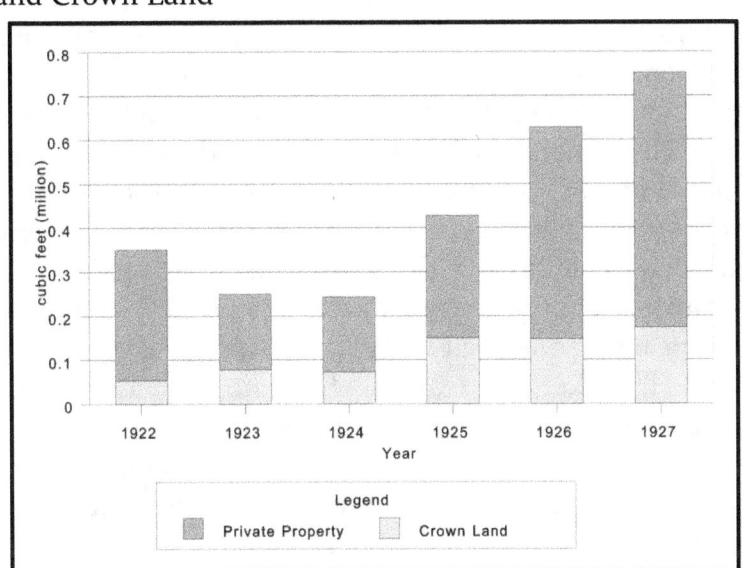

Forests Department Annual Reports 1922-1927

Rising unemployment in the late 1920s

Rising unemployment among Anglo-Australians from 1927 onwards drew more attention to the presence of southern Europeans, often concentrated in hewing groups in the timber industry. Complaints grew louder in the local press that hundreds of men, including returned soldiers, were out of work. In July 1927, the *West Australian* reported that delegates from the employment bureau claimed that the 'influx of foreigners' continued unabated, many of whom:

> appeared to have employment provided for them immediately on arrival to the exclusion of British subjects.

The increasing 'visibility' of these migrant workers did

not augur well for them. Frustrated by its inability to control cutting and hewing on private property, the Forests Department changed tack. Instead of blaming the depression that was sweeping the industry on the unregulated competition of those involved in the export of hewn sleepers, the Department turned its attention to the changing ethnic composition of the hewing workforce. It blamed Southern Europeans who were entering the industry - 'this small army of hewers'.

During the year to March 1927, 1,685 southern Europeans had arrived in Western Australia. According to E. H. Barker, secretary of the State Executive of the Australian Labour Party, 'this large number of aliens' caused a 'considerable amount' of the unemployment. Barker believed there was some organisation behind the importation of these men because:

> they were drafted to country districts almost as soon as they arrived. The foreigners, many of whom could not speak English, could often be seen waiting for country trains and for somebody in charge of them to supply them with tickets.

He denounced as 'callous and inhuman' the policy of dumping foreigners into the country when so much unemployment existed. In a letter to the Secretary of State for the Dominions, Barker wrote that:

> These men arrive in Western Australia and take work on wages and conditions which no Britisher would accept and are thereby tending to bring down the standard of living of the whole community ...the result being that thousands of Britishers are unable to secure employment.

In 1928, in response to enquiries by the League of

Nations with regard to 'disabilities' suffered by aliens, the Western Australian Premier wrote that:

> No obstacle is placed in the way of aliens who are desirous of obtaining work, with the exception that State moneys are not advanced through the Agricultural Bank or otherwise to farmers to employ Southern Europeans. In all other cases of country work Southern Europeans have an equal opportunity with Australians.

Yet just as sandalwood cutting had been restricted to British subjects despite there being no legislative provisions to this effect, so other discriminatory practices became the norm. In a letter to the British Migration Association, the Premier, echoing Barker's complaints, laid the blame for rising unemployment of British people on the presence of 'men of alien race':

> I venture to say that there would not be one idle man, who genuinely desires work, in Western Australia today if we did not have to contend with the competition, very often unfair, of men from Southern European countries, particularly Italians and Jugo-Slavs.

The lack of availability of other work placed these workers in an invidious position which could be exploited by unscrupulous sub-contractors, as Pietro Baruffi found to his dismay. Baruffi cut sleepers on private property in Bridgetown with two Rainoldi brothers, Sartorio and another two cutters working for an Anglo-Australian sub-contractor. The sleepers were carted to Hester siding with a team of horses and they would then be paid according to the number of sleepers which passed inspection. He was not paid for all the sleepers he had cut, 'too many sleepers short', and he complained unsuccessfully. It was not until much later that he found out that some of his sleepers were carted to Greenbushes instead of to Hester siding, stating:

> They get themselves, these guys, they used to cart the sleepers they ...fill up this wagon ...and every Saturday, 80 or 90 sleepers, they go down to Greenbushes ...they would brand them differently. When you cutting ... maybe six or seven cutters, six or seven brands ... and the bloke they cart sleepers they (take) some ... of your sleepers ...and who gonna think they gonna cart them blooming sleepers that far away.

Forestry regulations called for all hewers operating on Crown land to register their own brand; on private property, however, the owner would register a brand for all sleepers cut on his property. Giuseppe Palandri explained that each cutter had to be a registered timber worker and had his own brand (on the back side of the axe) to mark the sleepers he had cut. Whilst Mate Alac had his own brand 'MX' on the broad-axe which was recorded with the sub-contractor, he complained that:

> I've been exploited left and right. Not me, but everyone foreigner come here in this country ... exploited in a rotten way.

Italians and Croatians move into sleeper contracting

From around 1925 increasing number of Italians and Croatians took up sleeper contracting. Some of these exploited their own countrymen, often not paying them at all for the work performed. Both Stefania Rijavec and Elsie Radomiljac insisted that many of the sleeper cutters were not paid for all the sleepers they cut as they had moved on by the time the timber was taken away. In his home in Tuart Hill in 1995, Alac reflected:

> Many of the time they never pay you. True ...they never pay you and you quite worried, what you gonna do. You don't know language. You got no friend ...you got no money.

On another occasion, when Alac and a workmate went to a contractor to collect money due on sleepers, the contractor told them that he could not pay anything because 'your bloody sleepers no good'. According to Alac, his friend was so shocked that he collapsed, 'his legs give way on him'.

Elsie Radomiljac and S. Viskovich both stated that non-payment for sleepers was not unusual. However Elsie ensured that the cutters employed by her husband were always paid whilst Stefania Rijavec lamented on the ensuing poverty of many cutters who did not receive payment for their work:

> Sono portati il timber via... tanti andati via che ... sono lavorati per niente. Non l'ha pagate. [They took the timber away... many went away who...they had worked for nothing. They were not paid].

Many Italians and Croatians had borrowed money to cover the journey to Australia and to satisfy the landing money requirement of the Australian immigration authorities. The exploitation of sleeper cutters through non-payment for work therefore was an added hardship for these immigrants who needed the money to send home to their relations to repay their debts, to help out their families struggling back home, and to be able to live. Mate Alac had given two forty-pound cheques which he and a friend had brought to Australia under the landing money requirement to the first contractor, Ante Urlic (also known as Bilonja), for whom they worked in Harvey to convert to cash. They never saw the money:

> Bilonja hadn't given me the forty pounds nor pay for the three weeks I had worked on the farm and three months I had been cutting sleepers for him. No one could have been more disillusioned than I. If only he would pay me so I could send something to my relatives. It would have been as if I had risen from the dead.

The Urlic brothers, who started in sleeper contracting in 1923, went out of business in 1928 owing, roughly, about £10,000 to the cutters, storekeepers and property owners, and also for royalty. They were not prevented from embarking upon a similar business again. The sleeper cutters had no hold over them, and had no way by which they could recover the money owing to them.

On another occasion, Alac had been instructed to move from one paddock in Episton to Collie. On arrival, Loiner, an Australian contractor of French origin:

> told us there weren't any more orders for sleepers and there wouldn't be any work. He gave each one of us five pounds and said that when the sleepers arrived at the railway station and were passed by the inspector he would pay us the remainder. This five pounds was my first pay in Australia.

Work was hard to come by and, although Alac was reluctant to work for his own countrymen whom he believed were the worst 'exploiters', it was often necessary to take the risk because no other work was available. Desperate for work, Alac went to work for a fellow countryman at Bindi Bindi clearing farmland:

> How our people worked at this camp and what they put up with is almost impossible to believe. None of the workers were allowed to wear a watch to work. In the morning when we left the camp we had to carry water, food and tools. Sometimes it was quite a distance so we had to leave camp at dawn and work until lunch. No one would ever know the time. We would go to lunch when the *zuti pas* [yellow dog] cooeed. The food, all mixed up, was carried in a kerosene tin, but we had to eat something otherwise we would have died of hunger. At the end of the day we had to wait for the boss to cooee again before we could finish and go back to the camp. That way no one knew exactly how many hours anyone had worked. This work was nothing better than slaves did in earlier times.

With shrinking work opportunities, Italians and Croatians found it easier to take up hewing contracts on private property where they were often employers of fellow countrymen, other Europeans and Anglo-Australians. They won contracts from the timber companies or from the Western Australian Government Railways (WAGR). In 1928, the Kauri Timber Company, for example, contracted an Italian by the name of Sartori who employed 11 cutters in the Nannup District to hew timber, while the Western Australian Government Railways (WAGR) utilised the services of Edwin Rodda to cut sleepers from the same area. Millers Timber and Trading and Bunning Bros contracted both individuals and gangs of Italians and Croatians (through sub-contractors) to hew and supply sleepers. Many Italian and Croatian sleeper cutters bought their own trucks and carted sleepers and other material according to what was available at the time.

Naturalisation

Italians and Croatians who met the eligibility criteria for citizenship often resorted to naturalisation to overcome unemployment or increasing work restrictions imposed on aliens. Pietro Baruffi injured his knee whilst operating a crosscut saw and was advised by the doctor to 'find an easier job'. The Chairman of the Road Board advised him in 1926 to become naturalised as this would entitle him to more rights and to be able to move out of the hewing industry. To this, Baruffi responded 'I'm prepared to do anything' and immediately applied for naturalisation. Baruffi was naturalised on 18 February 1927, six years after his arrival in Western Australia. As the sleeper industry virtually came to a halt in mid-1927, Baruffi became interested in a block in Balingup abandoned by a returned soldier:

> government let me have the farm because I was naturalised. But if it is not naturalised in those days, they don't give any.

Baruffi moved on to the block and with his wife, Maria, set about clearing the farm with 'axe and shovel'. In this fashion, they gradually cleared the 215 acres. He took up dairy farming and moved from cutting sleepers to carting sleepers for timber exporters, Jackson and Rogers, who supplied him with the truck.

Public sentiment

The naturalisation status of Italians and Croatians did not influence perceptions of these groups who were

'White-anting the British Stock'   27

classified by immigration authorities as 'low-status'. In October 1928, the *Daily News* reported J. Mulqueeny, who represented the Returned Soldiers' Congress (Perth), stating that Italians and Croatians would 'white-ant the British stock'. He argued that they:

> did not possess the mentality of Australians. There is no reason why they should not be employed. They should do the coolie work and we should be the bosses.

Many of those interviewed pointed out that southern Europeans and Anglo-Australians did not mix socially. Ivan Surina went so far as to state that each nationality lived in separate camp sites as 'otherwise they would fight too much'. Dell'Agostino often joined his father and some of their Italian friends for a glass of brandy before breakfast. As they walked down the street his father warned him not to linger

> because ...might be dangerous. People come and start bashing you around.

They entered the local hotel only if there were not too many Australians around.

In Western Australia, Premier Phillip Collier was at the forefront in reinforcing negative ethnic stereotypes:

> We will continue to protect against this State being flooded with men whom we do not want, and whose presence is responsible for reducing the opportunities of employment for our own people.

Giuseppe Palandri stated that not many Anglo-Australians used to cut sleepers because the work and living conditions were too harsh. The desire of Italians and Croatians to own land and provide economic stability to their families was also a great incentive to work hard. However, most Italians and Croatians moved out of the industry when they became naturalised and could purchase land.

Very little support for the Italians and Croatians was expressed. Some Anglo-Australian settlers signed petitions which were presented to the Premier stating that they had employed these workers and found them to be honest and hard-working and always paid their debts for provisions at the local stores. B. Dell'Agostino, for example, remarked that he never encountered any difficulty in finding work at Sausett's mill in Nannup because he enjoyed the reputation of a 'good worker'. Letters to the same effect also surfaced in Western Australian local and regional newspapers. L. W. Le Quesne, Chairman of the Anglican Church Immigration Committee, stated in 1929:

> Southern Europeans could be admitted in not excessive numbers for they were particularly adapted to bush life and clearing and compared with the English migrant, were more suitable for this particular work.

Towards the end of the decade, and with the onset of the recession, the dreams of economic security that these immigrants had sought soured, expectation giving way to desperation.

Roelands Camp Site 1926 *(photo courtesy S. Viskovich)*

Hewing team at Roelands, 1926. Left to right (back row) unknown, M. Sumich, unknown; (second row) unknown, unknown, V.Nucih, M. Viskovich, S. Viskovich, K. Viskovich, M. Alac; (third row) ? Surach, K. Sunde, K. Sumich, F. Sumich, M. Sumich, K. Sumich, A. Misich; (front row) V. Bilcich, J. Jakich, J. Babich *(photo courtesy S. Viskovich)*

2

'Axes Swung by Aliens'

> 'Depression was for me from the beginning, when I come here. What they call depression... they call recession now, that's more easy.'
>
> Mate Alac (Interview).

The Depression years were harsh years for Italians and Croatians in the timber industry, more so for those who were not naturalised. From the late 1920s widespread unemployment among Anglo-Australians, the closing of doors to southern European immigration and greater work restriction further isolated these immigrant workers. These developments pushed some of them to extreme measures in their struggle to survive. Italians and Croatians found themselves increasingly under attack from all quarters.

End of the timber industry boom

The four-year boom in timber production which ended about the middle of 1928 was very much a repetition of the mild boom in sleeper exports of the early 1920s. To a large extent, it was due to the increase in hewn timber on private property principally, though not entirely, for sleepers. During this boom Western Australia exported more timber than in any other period before or up to the 1960s, accounting for over 10% of total exports of £15 million. Hewing operations fell off dramatically from the second half of the year causing considerable unemployment among sleeper hewers. The outcome was that by 1928 there was a huge sleeper stockpile and falling export revenue for sleepers, resulting in a great slackening in hewing operations and exceptionally low prices for hewers.

Timber hewing and migrant workers

In spite of growing unemployment among Anglo-Australians in 1928, a strong presence of Italians and Croatians in hewing continued. Foresters' reports show that in the Ludlow, Busselton, Margaret River and Yarloop district, hewing was confined to private property, where 'foreigners, mostly Slavs and Italians' carried out the bulk of the work. In March 1928, the Western Mail called for a 'Ban on foreign labour'. Settlers were urged to employ British labour in preference to 'foreigners' in clearing operations. Then in April 1928, the Minister for Agriculture issued a notice to remind District Inspectors of the Agricultural Bank that:

> the Minister will only grant permission to settlers to employ foreign labour where proof is forthcoming that British and Australian labour is not procurable.

This directive was acted upon by many settlers as Mate Alac found out to his dismay. Alac moved to the goldfields in 1929:

> I had lost hope of ever getting work. I no longer knew

the value of money as I had been without it for so long. I was lucky that I always read books and often forgot my hunger. A man without work in a foreign country is like a stray dog. No one wants you or wants to know you.

With his friend, Nikola Miocevic, Alac decided to travel to Meekatharra and Mullewa and was overjoyed to find that work was available on a farm at Tenindewa. However, when the settler found out that they were not British subjects, Alac and Miocevic were told 'no work'.

In August 1928, the *Daily News* reported that whilst Italian men had 'the right to work and obtain food and quarters', they had traversed the State meeting with 'closed doors' everywhere. A month later, the *Daily News* reported that unemployed Italians had approached the Unemployed Union asking for admittance or affiliation so that they could approach the government for relief and sustenance. They were told:

> they had enough to do to look after their own, without bringing in Southern Europeans.

The plight of Croatians was no better with the *West Australian* reporting 40% unemployed in 1929. Forests Department records show that, for example, in the Yarloop district, the hewing of sleepers was 'practically in the hands of foreigners, mostly Jugo-slavs' who were not earning more than 'tucker'. In the words of Mate Alac:

> contractor got permit from the government, but then, most of the time they had to let go their regulation because they didn't have the workers to do job, so the non-British or foreigners workers they doing the work without being naturalised and all that, but when it

comes to strict rules ...like the government railway sleepers they couldn't do it unless they were naturalised and they were British subjects.

Non-naturalised Italians and Croatians accepted whatever work was available. With no protection afforded to them against underpayment of piecework or wages, and often with no other work to go to, it is not surprising that their numbers in clearing operations and in hewing on private properties increased wherever they could find work, regardless of pay and conditions that were offered. A. Lurara, of the Club Giovane Italia, commented that the refusal of the Unemployed Union to accept Italians into their ranks:

> did nothing to the union's credit because, by doing so, they ...left the Italians to starve and to scab.

The Forests Department

Eleven years after starting operations, the Forests Department was well positioned for its second decade of forest management. Although it had failed in its bid to establish control of hewing on private property, the onset of the depression served it well. It slowed down the rate of forest exploitation. At the same time the Department had significantly increased the area of state forest to preserve the 'immensely valuable forest heritage' (Refer Map 2).

Timber production continued its dramatic slide into the early 1930s and many timber mills found it necessary to close. The number of men employed in sawmills fell substantially, with many employees working only part-time and on reduced wages. In contrast, although hewn timber production from private property dominated by Italians and Croatians had fallen considerably since 1927, it had levelled out in 1929. Hewn timber production gradually increased in the years to June 1931 to the consternation of the Forests Department (Figure 2.1).

Figure 2.1: Hewn timber production from Crown land and from private property in relation to the total timber production

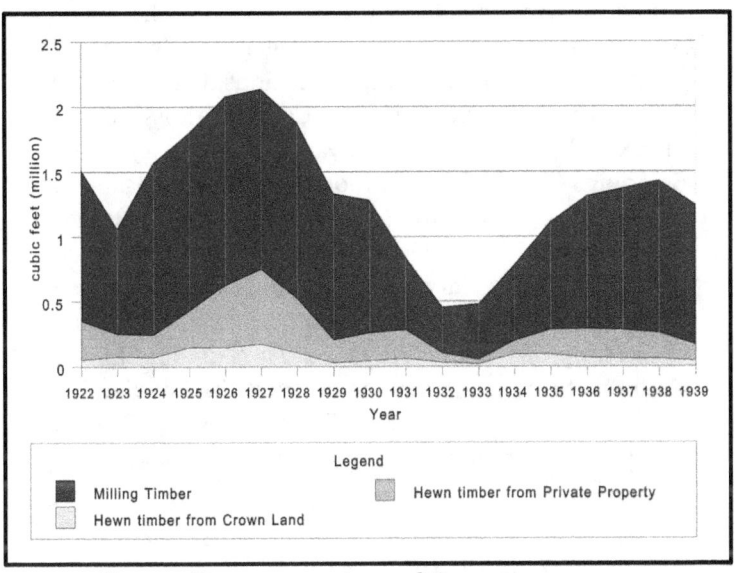

Forests Department Annual Reports 1922-1939

By 1930, accumulated stocks of sleepers built over the years had been cleared, but the overseas markets had been supplied with large quantities of jarrah sleepers at below production costs. The Forests Department came under increasing pressure from all quarters to release more land and keep timber workers employed. Instead, the department complained that:

> The bulk of the sleepers for the export trade came from private property, where practically the whole of the hewing is in the hands of Southern Europeans who

have forced the old experienced hewers out of the export business.

In fact, a sleeper consignment for the South African government on board the s.s. *Erica* in 1931 listed the sub-contractors as:

> Balingup, Anduchich; Yarloop, Antunovich; Beela, Alach; Harvey, Butorax; Wagerup, Bukranich; Balingup, Bilich; Kirup, Bilich; Roelands, Beros; Benger, Boyanich; Collie and Bulading, Colli and Rossi; Boyup Brook, C.R. Doust; Darkin, Evas; Bunbury, Gavranich; Bulading, Ivicevich; Brookhampton, Kostanich; Dardanup, Jiovanoni; Burekup, Marchesi; Greenbushes, Marovich; Waroona, Miranovich; Darkin, Miloth; Harvey, Panjrich; Lowden, Plecash; Roelands, Pavlinovich; Donnybrook, Rondvich; Cookernup, Radovich; Wilga, Sokal; Nannup, Stanich; Nannup, Seman; Harvey, Stanich; Balingup, Sumich; Bunbury, Sakich; Hester, Tucak; Hester, Tonich; Margaret River, Tucak; Roelands, Ungdegak; Muja, Zadkovich.

Immigration restrictions

With spiralling unemployment, the public demanded greater restriction of work opportunities to these immigrant workers. Questions were raised in the Western Australian State Parliament proposing that 'migrants from Southern Europe be discouraged, stopped or regulated'. Agreement was reached with the Italian government in 1928 to restrict the number of immigrants to 3,000 a year by using a system of nomination papers (Atto di Chiamata) and limiting the number of passports issued with visas to Australia. In addition, the 1,200 quota for Yugoslavs, among others, was halved in mid-1928 and halved again in the following year. In 1929, the quota for Italians was reduced to 1,500 close relatives, namely wives and children of those who were naturalised.

In response to persistent calls to put a stop to Italian and Croatian immigration, the Federal Government introduced more immigration restrictions in late 1930. The dictation test was applied to prohibit entry to Italians who arrived on two boats, with the Australian government claiming that the Italian authorities were not adhering to their agreement on restricting immigration to Australia. Then towards the end of that year, the federal government closed the doors to all southern Europeans except close dependent relatives of persons already settled in Australia or persons who had considerable financial means of their own.

Spiralling unemployment

Antagonism towards foreign timber workers peaked in 1929. The crash in the timber export trade drove sleeper prices down and left a huge stockpile of sleepers. In December 1929, Croatian cutters working near Darkin mill disobeyed a Timber Union directive and kept on cutting in the hope of selling the sleepers. Stipe Viskovich described how he and his work mates had gone to Perth for Christmas and there they received a phone call from the farmer to inform them that their sleepers were burning at the siding. Union men had gone out and set fire to about £300-£400 worth of sleepers because, whereas farmers were paid an allowance for clearing the land, cutters were paid only when the sleepers were sold. The Timber Union found out that many of the Croatians were still cutting sleepers and put a stop to this by destroying the sleepers. A distressed Pietro Baruffi stated that the Croatians were poor, desperate people trying to earn 'a few bob ...to carry on cutting sleepers' in the hope that the sleeper export business would pick up once again.

As the ranks of the unemployed increased from 13.8% in 1929/30 to 24.1% in 1930/31, Anglo-Australians expressed their frustration though public protest directed at Italians and Croatians. The *West Australian* reported in September 1931 soldier settlers' complaints that 'foreign timber workers' threatened their livelihood. Their anger erupted at the Soldier Settlers' Conference in 1931 with Mr Walker (Mundaring Branch) stating:

> Committees have been formed ...to keep our own people off the breadline, while the forests ring with axes swung by aliens. ...The foreigners lived on practically nothing and sent most of their money out of the country. They are no asset to the State... and the Government would be doing a service if it took them out of the bush and replaced them with our own men.

The result was a motion calling for an amendment of the *Forests Act* to permit only 'natural-born and naturalised British subjects' to register for employment in the industry. This move was aimed at excluding aliens from obtaining any form of work such as fallers, timber carters and firewood cutters, all of which came under the jurisdiction of the Forests Department.

Growing restrictions for Italian and Croatian timber workers

In response to public demands to restrict employment to British subjects, a number of measures were implemented. In July 1931, forestry regulations were amended so that, in producing sleepers for the government railways:

> No person not being a natural-born or naturalised British subject shall be employed by the contractor or any sub-contractor ...unless British subjects are not available for employment.

Two months later, the *West Australian* reported that cutting firewood production would be similarly restricted. The Forests Department extended this control to include all timber production from group settlement schemes.

The public outcry against Italian and Croatian timber workers had facilitated the Forests Department's efforts to finally curtail hewing activity on private property - its greatest bane. It now reported that it took much longer to properly inspect sleepers obtained from private property due to:

> the number of delays occasioned by inefficiency and at times deliberate interference by foreign turners' (timber turners turned the timber over for inspection).

In 1932, the fee for inspecting sleepers on private property was raised by fifty percent. Arguing that this step was necessary to protect the interest of British workers and the sleeper-hewing industry, the Minister for Forests warned that:

> intense competition and the exploitation of foreign labour have brought the overseas price of hewn sleepers down to a ruinously low level. ...Experienced British cutters have been ousted from the industry by newly arrived foreigners, who have no dependents in the country and are prepared very often to work for a remuneration which would make it absolutely impossible for an Australian to maintain a wife and

> family in food alone... Many of the foreigners were indifferent cutters. These men are ruining our own men and our industry.

This increase in fee served to make hewing on private property unattractive. The Minister for Forests and the Forests Department both acknowledged that exploitation of Italians and Croatians had taken place:

> Possibly, the individual private property owner does not realise that, in allowing his timber to be cut by foreigners, he is in effect exploiting the hewn sleeper market to the detriment of the timber industry and the State as a whole.

One can but speculate that the two most likely outcomes of this action would have been to (a) discourage private property owners from hewing sleepers for export as this was no longer profitable and (b) put more pressure on the prices that these owners were likely to pay to immigrant labour already precariously situated at the periphery of the labour market. It certainly did not encourage private property owners to employ Anglo-Australians in their stead. In fact, the *Collie Mail,* reported that at a rowdy public meeting in Collie in March 1933, Anglo-Australian timber workers denounced the extensive powers held by the Conservator of Forests. They protested that the Conservator had absolute control of the industry 'even to the matter of employment of cutters'. The Collie timber workers complained that the Forests Department often threw land open to cutters that was so inferior in timber quality that up to 14% of the sleepers cut were condemned, the loss being carried by the cutters. They complained:

many dinkum sleeper cutters had built homes out of their earnings in the past, and now they find they cannot get decent timber near their homes to allow them to scratch for a living.

According to the protesters, the Forests Department needed to reverse its 'forestry grab' policy and release a small belt of timber land in particular districts to help licenced cutters. The protesters had moved a motion to obtain:

> better bush to cut the export sleepers from; a reduction in the amount of the royalty charges and inspection fees charges; a less rigid inspection of sleepers before cutters get payment; a provision that rejected sleepers become the property of the sleeper-cutter and carter.

The (Anglo-Australian) cutters also demanded that the reduction of these fees be passed to the timber workers and not to the contractors, timber companies or their agents. In the Western Australian parliament, J. H. Smith, MLA (Nelson), joined the voices of criticism directed at the Forests Department:

> the unemployment position was as acute now as it had ever been. Through the Forests Department, the Government greatly exploited those engaged in the timber industry.

The height of the Depression in the timber industry

As the depression reached its most severe point in the timber industry in 1932-1933, hewn timber production fell to its lowest ebb in the interwar period. Increased inspection fees also had the desired effect of restricting hewing activity on private property. The result was devastating to registered timber workers as the number of employed in the industry dropped to 803 by June 1932, a fall of approximately 60% from 2,340 in 1930.

Although in policy there was no distinction between natural-born or naturalised British subjects, naturalised Italians and Croatians were classified as 'naturalised foreigners'. These workers recognised an unwritten code of preference. Reflecting Giuseppe Palandri's view, Albert Piacentini believed that although his father was naturalised it was understandable that 'the native population had priority'. Aliens, of course, were at the bottom of the hierarchy. Other Italian and Croatian timber workers were far from passive about their situation. Apart from the option of return migration, Italians in particular complained to their consul.

Italian and Croatian Migration

Adverse economic conditions and restricted work opportunities prompted many to return to their countries of origin. In fact there was a net migration loss of 1,008 between 1929 and 1934 in Western Australia (Table 2.1).

Figures for Croatian migration to Western Australia are not available, although national figures show a net migration loss for 'Jugoslavs' of 485 for the years 1929-1934. The 1933 Australian Bureau of Statistics census showed that there were over 700 Italians and Croatians in the south-west land division, with Harvey recording the highest number of Italians (114) and Yugoslavs (34) followed by Manjimup (44 Italians and 31 Yugoslavs).

Women and Children

The proportion of female Italian immigrants steadily increased after 1933, the majority coming as wives and fiancées. For example, Carlo Bertelli brought out his wife and three sons in 1934. There was a similar increase in female immigration for Yugoslavs from the early 1930s, and Mate Alac recalled that many Croatians 'bring their wives or girls here'. Cvitko (Charlie) Ucich brought out his wife, his two sons and two daughters in 1936. However, a different perspective was put forward by E. Radomiljac who commented that:

> Most of the Italians as soon as they possibly could, they brought their families over... the wives or the girlfriends, got married and settled down, but the Yugoslavs didn't bring the women folk over the same. They sent money over to them and very few that I know of brought their wives over here.

A similar view was expressed by Joan Ladhams who stated that many Yugoslavs 'only stayed here until they were old men and then packed up and left'. According to Giuseppe Palandri:

> the Italian couldn't live over there and they had it good over here... but I think the Yugoslav must have been ...living pretty good over there or they thought it was better, and instead of bringing their wives out, they all went back.

Census figures for 1933 support S. Viskovich's view that those Croatians who were naturalised and had earned enough to purchase land moved on to vineyards in the Swan valley or market gardens in Spearwood and Osborne Park. Italians, on the other hand, tended to settle in the Manjimup-Margaret River area. This probably accounted for the different perceptions with regard to bringing families to Western Australia.

Table 2.1: Italian Migration (Western Australia) 1929 - 1939

Year	Arrivals			Departures			*Net Migration
	Males	Females	Total	Males	Females	Total	
1929	416	170	586	469	44	513	73
1930	330	113	443	781	64	845	-402
1931	135	99	234	879	34	913	-679
1932	111	91	202	355	21	376	-174
1933	189	126	315	214	24	238	77
1934	203	165	368	215	56	271	97
1935	325	233	558	125	32	157	401
1936	252	238	490	140	23	163	327
1937	548	270	818	169	8	217	601
1938	931	357	1,288	232	38	270	1,018
1939	479	287	766	139	51	190	576

(*Excess of arrivals over departures) Western Australian Statistical Register

Wages and work compensation

One of the anomalies hewers faced was that, unlike other timber workers such as fallers, they were often treated as contractors and therefore stood unprotected. The result was that, by 1931, fallers and broad-axe men were covered by a timber industry wages award which stipulated their margin as 15s. and 26s. respectively over the base rate of £4.7s. per week. In contrast, hewers were being paid as little as 10s. a load, which often took up to four or five days to produce due to the poor nature of the bush that was released.

T. Moore (ALP), MLC (Central District) contended

that, whilst hewers worked side by side with:

> piecework fallers ...working in the same country, for the same people, and under the same conditions

they could not enjoy the same benefit of a minimum rate to which fallers were entitled. Moore claimed that it was unfair competition that had cut rates for hewers and that 'the wily foreigners' were to blame for this exploitation. A number of articles in the *West Australian* in November 1934 echoed Moore's views whilst acknowledging that sleeper hewers 'were being harassed under slave-like conditions'.

May Holman (ALP), MLA (Forrest) spoke out in State Parliament about the plight of the sleeper hewers, pointing out that:

> the worker ...is forced to cut sleepers at any rate, the man ...has no award rate under which to work, the man ...cannot get his money, not even by going to the courts.

Holman argued that the 1923 Amendment to the *Workers' Compensation Act* showed beyond doubt that the hewer had always been recognised as a piece worker and not a contractor. She defended the Italians and Croatians as victims of circumstance and exploitation. Arguing that the nature of work in sleeper cutting entailed working either singly or in small isolated groups throughout the south-west forests, she stated:

> Sleeper cutters - particularly foreigners ...are easily beguiled to sign away all their rights without knowing what they are doing. Often they have been compelled to sign a paper ...before they can get work at all. Documents are signed by men in entire ignorance and

by which they cease to be workers and are deprived of the wage for their labour.

Holman termed these contracts which deprived 'foreign sleeper cutters' of their right to sue for wages as 'pure chicanery'. The amount of money earned by cutters and not paid to them was conservatively estimated to be in the region of £50,000. In fact the *West Australian* reported in January 1933 that unscrupulous sub-contractors frequently 'absconded' without paying the men anything for the work done.

Neither was the exploitation of Italians and Croatians in the timber industry restricted to sleeper hewing. Clearers were sometimes left unpaid even though the farmer himself had received his clearing advances from the Agricultural Bank. Mate Alac recounted how several of his friends had not been paid for clearing a farm by the farmer who claimed he did not have the money to pay them. He told me how this farmer, however, could afford the £5 fee to pay the policeman for evicting the clearers making their pay claim. Exploitation of labour by 'Slavs and people who were working in the timber industry' was acknowledged in parliament with A.A. Wilson (ALP), MLA (Collie), reporting that:

> Instances are quite common in the South-west of poor devils who, after working for three or four months, have been unable to get a penny of their wages from these unscrupulous employers.

It was often dismissed as a practice 'indulged in largely amongst foreigners'. Yet Wilson pointed out that:

> although many of the unscrupulous employers do come from foreign countries... it may be well to state that it is not foreigners only who have taken the timber

workers down. Some of the British and Australian-born are the worst scoundrels of the lot.

Self-mutilation

Italians and Croatians endured harsh conditions but it was the inability to earn a reasonable wage or even, at times, to find work drove these immigrant workers to take drastic action. Self-mutilation, usually in the form of chopping off fingers and toes, to obtain a workers' compensation payout, increased dramatically during the depression with aliens, naturalised workers and Anglo-Australians participating in this practice. The number of these claims rose dramatically from the late 1920s. In the Yarloop district, for example, four claims were made under the *Workers' Compensation Act* in 1929. Forests Department records show:

> In one case that appeared genuine a fellow countryman of the claimant informed (after compensation had been paid) that four toes were cut off intentionally; that the man was lazy and would not work and wanted the money to go home to his country.

The great increase in the number of Workers' Compensation claims was also of concern to the immigrant timber workers. As forester Gallager pointed out:

> In talking to some of these foreigners who appear to be honest and genuine, they are beginning to realise so many accidents and compensation claims are beginning to react against them.

Josie Carzoli told me that many cases of workers' compensation claims were genuine, 'because crosscut saws and broad-axes were very dangerous', especially to newcomers to the industry, whatever their nationality. Dell'Agostino, Ucich, Palandri, Viskovich, Bertelli, and Alac had all either experienced some injury or had witnessed or just avoided some horrific accident. Dell' Agostino worked at the mill in Nannup whenever work was available but when, in 1934, he was offered work as a hookman, he quit. A hookman worked the logs on the landing. The logs would be rolled up on to 'skids' to load them on to the railway carts. Dell' Agostino believed the landing at Nannup was too steep and dangerous and had reported this to the foreman only to be ignored. In his words:

> It must be my Lord look after me...because he stop me to work the landing and a fellow went up, he was a bit of a hookman too, because it's danger work that, it's good money...but... he went up, four days after he got killed. See, the log rolled back.

It was only then that the landing was pulled down and reconstructed.

One story repeated by several people (Story related by G. Palandri, S. Viskovich, B. Dell'Agostino, L. Bertelli and C. Coli.) was of the hewer who chopped off the toes of his left foot and, lying in bed in hospital, was asked by suspicious insurance authorities to produce the boot. When a friend produced it, the wrong boot had been cut and the scam was confirmed. However, the ethnicity of the culprits often changed according to who was telling the story, probably because they worked with their own countrymen. Dell' Agostino claimed he knew of three or four Italians who had cut toes and fingers off, 'not the little finger, he cut some of the other fingers' (pointing to the thumb, index and ring fingers). Alac, on the other hand, spoke out about some Croatians, all from the same island in Dalmatia, who indulged in this practice:

> There were thirty-four (from this island)...in Western Australia and thirty-three had cut off their toes. There were many others from Yugoslavia who also did this.

Alac was an unwitting eyewitness to one such account of self-mutilation when he came upon two Croatians one of whom had cut off the thumb of his friend, stating that it 'flew like a grasshopper'. He found it difficult to accept that some of his fellow Croatians could take this action, stating that 'some would cut off four toes on one foot and leave the big toe; others would cut off all five'. He recalled that 'good few Italians cut their toes' and Anglo-Australians 'cut plenty toes too'. Alac nevertheless sympathised with the hardship that drove men to mutilate themselves in order to get insurance money, stating:

> In order to raise their fare and the necessary cash, these men often borrowed ...at exorbitant interest rates. Generally the £40 was returned immediately work was found. ...A considerable portion of these men were married and in addition to meeting the usurers' requirements also had an obligation to send money home to support their families.

Many Italians and Croatians had left families in their countries of origin who were struggling to survive. To such people, the landing money requirement simply made life more difficult as they shouldered more debts to meet costs. Ivan Kurusin migrated to Australia to be able to provide for his wife and children. He did not have the money for the passage or for the landing money requirement and had to borrow £80 at 50% interest from a returned migrant who had done well in the USA. Kurusin told me:

> He gave me eighty pounds, but I had signed for £120 as the twelve months interest was included. I have to return the money within a period of two years with interest. If I don't pay within the two years, he will take all my holdings. When that happens, my wife and children will be thrown out, without house or home.

S. Viskovich related the story of a Croatian who cut his toes off in desperation and then sent his wife the insurance payout, so that 'his wife had the money and the maggies (magpies) had his toes'. Some needed the money for the journey home and yet others used the money to move out of hewing. The workers' compensation payout for one finger in a particular case was used to purchase a truck, according to Basileo Dell'Agostino. However, others questioned the practice of self-mutilation. In Bertelli's words:

> Once you lose your finger, you haven't got another one. Once you chuck your foot off, you don't have a foot.

Bunning Bros' 1938 Annual Report challenges the perception that Italians and Croatians were the worst perpetuators of fraudulent workers' compensation claims:

> Several big accident payouts happened in this period under review, and other than the finger loss cases, were genuine accidents. The feature of the finger loss cases was that all the men were Britishers, a fact that lessens the doubt that may have existed, were the men foreigners.

This is confirmed by Table 2.2 which shows the nationality of persons injured and the number of persons engaged in the timber industry.

Table 2.2: Number of notifiable accidents in 1930 by nationality

Nationality of Persons Injured	Total	%
British	453	92.3
Italian	25	5.1
Slav	1	0.2
Other European	12	2.4
TOTAL	491	100.0
Approx. No. of persons engaged in industry	2,340	

Compiled from Forests Department Annual Report 1931

Unions

Many Italian and Croatian timber workers joined the timber workers union in the 1930s. At a meeting in Bunbury in 1933, J. Thomas, organiser of the Western Australian Timber Workers' Union, criticised some sleeper contractors who had exploited the ethnicity of timber workers, observing:

> It is remarkable that certain contractors are now so anxious to employ Australian cutters, as for years past they have only employed foreign cutters, but, until recently, these men were disorganised and did not know as much as they do to-day, hence the sudden sympathy and the attempts being made to use the Australian cutters as a lever to break up the solidarity of the workers as a whole.

Thomas acknowledged the contribution of Italian and

Croatian timber workers in the sleeper hewing dispute over non-payment and piece rates. Urging members not to allow employers to divide their ranks on the basis of nationality, he pointed out that:

> overseas cutters had put up a great fight not only for themselves, but for British cutters.

As the depression took its toll, many Italians and Croatians turned to whatever opportunity was available to secure their livelihood as will be seen in the next chapter.

3

Survival: Naturalisation and Mobility

Italians and Croatians responded to the ever-shrinking work opportunities in two main ways, namely naturalisation and mobility often with the two combined. The depression years had seen many Italians and Croatians return to their native lands. Many of those who stayed behind chose to take up citizenship as Table 3.1 shows.

Table 3.1: Naturalisation

	1929	1930	1931	1932	1933	1934	1935	1936	1937	1938	193
It*	172	313	185	136	121	144	145	103	56	80	125
Yu*	79	275	95	106	92	88	72	20	25	24	40

(*Italians and Yugoslavs) Western Australian Statistical Registers

Naturalisation often meant the difference in their ability to survive. Figures for 1930 almost doubled as many Italians and Croatians took this option as soon as they had completed five years' residence in Australia. Stipe Viskovich had migrated to Australia in 1926 and became naturalised in 1931. He explained:

> Well, in those days, if you are not Australian citizen you can't get any job in the government... it was hard to get any government job.

Viskovich was working for a contractor on the Main Roads Board when the timber workers' union discovered that he was not naturalised and protested. As he had been in Australia for five years, the contractor suggested that he apply for naturalisation in order to be able to retain his job. Viskovich immediately applied and became naturalised. He told me:

> it was difficult only for a migrant. In those days, only sleeper cutting or woodline.

This was a view shared by Ivan Surina, who stated:

> if you stranger, you have to be naturalised...if you not naturalised, you got nothing.

During the depression years, naturalisation also ensured better access to sustenance work. Non-naturalised Italians and Croatians faced uncertain prospects. Responding to enquiries by the Vice-consul for Italy in 1932, the secretary of the Unemployment Board in Western Australia wrote:

> I have your letter ...intimating that you had been informed by some Italians that sustenance has been discontinued owing to their not being British subjects. Failure to obtain naturalisation has not debarred Italians from receiving sustenance nor has any distinction been exercised, but it is considered that, in view of the harvest work offering in the country, opportunities exist for employment to be secured.

Most Italians and Croatians who were given sustenance work were employed as clearers. Albert Piacentini described one of the sustenance camps with 50 or 60 men near Bunbury. Under the supervision of a foreman, the men worked on abandoned farms, ringbarking trees and clearing the land:

> People used to get ...one and a half days a week or two days a week work. They'd take it on rotation. There was a huge number of people without jobs and the government...used to try and assist.

Cvitko (Charlie) Ucich, naturalised in 1932, was offered periodic clearing work with the Nannup Road Board. Carlo Bertelli, naturalised in 1936, still worked on and off at Lyall's mill near Collie during the early 1930s, depending on the availability of work. He also worked for the government ringbarking trees for 10 shillings a week during times of unemployment. At the Italian Club in Bunbury in 1995, Vince Nani recalled some of his father's experiences stating that many received only 'seven bob a week ...just to dig sites ...to make a living'.

Non-naturalised unemployed aliens could apply for a meal ticket which entitled them to one meal a day but, according to some of the interviewees, many 'missed out'. 'Some people didn't have it and some did,' Stipe Viskovich recalled. Unemployment benefits did not exist in the interwar period so that, for many non-naturalised immigrants, 'if you work you live, if you didn't work, no living'.

Mobility

Mobility was an important survival strategy for aliens, but did not always yield the results that were desired, often causing great hardship and anxiety. As mentioned earlier, mobility entailed return migration for some. For those who stayed in Western Australia, some moved within the timber industry and others between industries.

Mate Alac often covered great distances shifting from the south-west timber industry to the goldfields and to the agricultural areas where clearing needed to be done. Alac moved back to the timber industry in 1938 for a short time before returning to the goldfields. Stipe Viskovich worked in Boddington, Harvey, Waroona, Greenbushes and Darkin, wherever he 'could find work'. He moved from hewing to carting around Cue in 1929 whilst also prospecting for gold. In 1934, Viskovich moved on to a vineyard in Millendon, where he lived in 1995 in retirement.

According to Elsie Radomiljac, living in a retirement cottage in Manjimup in 1995, her husband Marco had moved in the opposite direction, going from the wheat belt to Donnybrook, Kirup and Collie before finally settling at Manjimup. There, he turned to carting potatoes instead of sleepers and his payment was a bag of potatoes for every trip he made to the market. In Radomiljac's view, this was very fortunate as potatoes were not readily available, 'especially for foreigners, too'. Giacomo Palandri returned to Italy and to his wife to see if conditions there were any better. He re-emigrated to Western Australia in 1936 and resumed work in the timber industry. Mate Alac stated that he would have returned to Croatia if he had had the money. Perhaps Stefania Rijavec summed it up for most. In her words:

> Venuti ...perche trovano meglio un posto com'e stato la, invece e venuto piu male qui come siamo stati li, sotto fascismo. [They came ...because they find a better place

than it was back there, instead they ended up worse than back there, under fascism].

Some fared better than others. Luigi Bertelli claimed that, whilst times were tough, nobody 'went hungry'. Many naturalised Italians and Croatians such as Pietro Baruffi and Basileo Dell' Agostino acquired farms. Dell'Agostino grew 'spuds' on his farm in Gwelliup, near Nannup, which he bought in 1930. He also did:

> a bit on the farm and a bit on the mill...everywhere I could get a job because the job hard to get...if I could get a bit of money to keep the family going.

Dell'Agostino stated that for those on the land survival was easier than for those who depended on the availability of employment:

> Oh yes, there was a lot of people but...all poor. I got some ...cabbage, a few onion ...and I used to give them away for two penny, three penny for half a dozen. You cannot sell them because poor bugger they got no money. The father and mother ...and maybe five kid ...was working for five shillings a day...how can they live?

Others, like Bertelli, were adamant that conditions were not so desperate:

> Anybody who is starving in Australia, look, I don't care what anybody tells me, because we come in Australia, me father ...well, he didn't have anything. And he was getting 7 shillings or 10 shillings a week. But me father, he had a couple of gardens, he growing all the vegetables, he had chooks, or fowl or whatever you call them anyway, and ...the money he had, he used to use it for food. And if he had any to spare, well... we always

had wine there. To eat, we had plenty to eat.

Living conditions: the women

Living conditions for Italians and Croatians varied considerably. Single men were more able to move between locations and usually lived in tents. On arrival to join her husband Carlo in 1934, Luiga Bertelli and her two sons moved into 'not even a wooden house', but more of a shack that consisted of face cuts from the mill. Piacentini's father was luckier than most. He came to an arrangement with the Agricultural Bank to rent an abandoned group settlement house in Warner Glen where he was cutting sleepers. Giulio Carzoli and his wife, Josie, rented a room with the Italian contractor Marcelli for a few months after they got married in 1932. When Carzoli shifted to the Manjimup district to cart logs, he moved into a tent with an attached lean-to with his wife and two daughters.

Conditions were especially hard on some of the wives of timber workers, most of whom had no option but to follow their husbands wherever work was available. Elsie Radomiljac found it was a hard life living in a tent in the bush outside Donnybrook, 'ten miles from anybody' with a baby. As this was the first of her thirteen children, Elsie knew 'nothing about babies'. She related how:

> you came out of hospital and went straight down into the bush. Well you didn't know the first or the last thing to do ...tilly lamps ...candles... used to carry water from the well, because you were always out of a camp where there was water, used to carry that in. I used to carry Charlie on one hip and the bucket of water on the other one, because I didn't like to leave him in the camp, I was frightened somebody might pick him up.

She lamented that they were constantly shifting from one place to another. Her husband would come and tell her that they had finished cutting the timber and would shift camp the next day, so that:

> you had to pack everything up, you'd probably just got your nappies washed...and hanging on the line and then you had to go take them all in and fold them up. (In winter...) I used to dry them inside. I used to put the string across...because you had an open fire at one end. I managed, and my babies were never sick.

The burden on women was not restricted to harsh living conditions and child rearing. During the depression, Baruffi was sick for several years and Maria, his wife, had to get up at 3.00 am with the hurricane lamp and milk the cows, a job which was done by hand in those days. At her home in Gelorup in 1995, Nellie Giacci, recalled the tough times her mother, Maria, went through:

> She had to keep us all fed and clothed and a bit of food on the table. Mum had to take over. She always grew a few potatoes, vegetables... a few tomatoes, spinach. She planted a lot of fruit trees around. She was a great gardener, she pushed things into the ground and they grew. She grew buck wheat to make the polenta. Later on she used to grind the buckwheat. They'd send the buckwheat flour to sell. There would always be buckwheat flour flying around.

Nellie Giacci recounted how her mother, Maria Baruffi, also had to cope with her lack of knowledge of the English language. To go shopping, she walked four or five miles to the food store in Bridgetown and pointed at things she wanted. When the bag was full she would say

'*Basta, basta!*' [enough, enough!]. The lady in the shop would misunderstand thinking that she was being sworn at, and would scream back at her to Maria Baruffi's bewilderment.

Zuva Telenta came to Western Australia in 1930 to join her husband who was cutting sleepers at Boyup Brook. As well as doing all the cooking, washing, mending and cultivating of vegetables, Zuva, a physically strong woman, soon joined her husband and his mates cutting and sorting timber. When she returned from hospital after the birth of their first son in 1931, Zuva was amazed to discover that her husband had dismissed his co-workers because 'she was to be the only mate for their site'.

Lack of tolerance for other cultures also extended to those entering inter-cultural marriages as Elsie Radomiljac and Josie Carzoli, both of Anglo-Australian background, found out. After marrying a Croatian against her father's wishes, Elsie Radomiljac was shunned by many of her former friends and did not mix much with Anglo-Australians. Radomiljac noted that:

> the British were really funny towards foreigners at that time. They used to be standoffish (and) felt that they were better than anybody else.

Josie Carzoli faced a number of obstacles and objections from her father and sister because she wanted to marry an Italian. Despite the opposition, she married Giulio Carzoli in 1932.

Living conditions: Children

Bertelli and Ucich came out to Western Australia as children. Bertelli went straight to work on a farm, because his father couldn't afford to buy a bike for him to go to school which was nine miles away, too far to walk. Those who did attend school often had to contend with long walks in all types of weather. Ucich walked six miles to school every morning, joined by Bruno and Irene Bana about two miles into the trip. Within six months he could read and write a reasonable amount of English, recalling that:

> it was tough for a start... It was hard. Well, doing anything was hard.

Attending school also presented its problems. Carzoli recalled that it was hardest for her children who 'got ribbed a bit at school' and would be called names such as 'dagos'. Maria Nani's school recollections were such that she refused to be interviewed. According to her husband, Maria had:

> the roughest time that's possible because she was an Italian. She was treated like a bloody *zingara* [gypsy], and she went through hell.

In contrast, at school, Cesare Coli was lucky to meet one of the Bertellis who offered to look after him until he learnt to speak English. Esther Coli recalled that Australians were very biased against Italians and they were often teased at school 'because they were Catholic'.

Muted voices and Prejudice

All my informants recalled having been called 'dings' or 'dagos' at one time or other. Yet when the interview transcripts were sent to them for editing, they expressed the wish to delete or moderate accounts of specific incidents of conflict or victimisation that had been related during the taped interviews, even though these occurred over sixty years ago. Where general incidents were included, many insisted that they enjoyed good relations with individual Anglo-Australians who either employed them or worked with these groups, forming lasting friendships. Dell'Agostino, Surina and Baruffi believed that Australians were 'more against' the Italians and they learnt to keep their distance. Baruffi's general recollection of the interwar period was that Italians were very ill-treated by returned soldiers in particular. He felt that he had to be careful when going into a pub because:

> a lot of these young people they come back from the first world war...ask for trouble. They start insulting you and they want you to shout a drink for them. If you can afford and willing, that's alright. If you can't afford, they even spit in your bloody glass.

Most incidents of conflict occurred away from the workplace and at social gatherings such as dances or in hotels where Italians and Croatians could not avoid meeting Anglo-Australians.

Croatians shared similar experiences. At his home in Harvey in 1995, Ucich remembered how they were always having fights 'because they used to call us dagos'. He qualified this by stating that there were no strong feelings of rancour. In Elsie Radomiljac's view, relations with Anglo-Australians were strained and the different ethnic groups tended to stick together with their own countrymen to avoid conflict.

Giacomo Palandri and others rationalised matters differently. Palandri was not overly concerned with being called a 'ding'. According to his son Giuseppe:

> they call you dingo, but they don't even know what the

word means, because dingo (is) ...from the Spanish, *dego*... it's a well-up person... well, we call the English, pom... so what's the difference?

Palandri thought that the Australians were 'more intolerant than racist', arguing that times were tough for everyone and this made the Australians less helpful than they otherwise might have been.

Bertelli's perspective is probably the best example of the contradiction so often apparent in the interviews. On the one hand, Luigi Bertelli believed that it was up to immigrants to gain acceptance, expressing the view that many Italians did not 'get on' with Australians. He had not felt restricted by the attitude of Australians and by the name calling, and he and his brother were:

> always going out together. We were bike riding, playing sports, you know, all the time, soccer, football. We played cricket. Actually we used to go for the night in Collie, we had no trouble at all, all mates.

When personally confronted, however, Bertelli's response was quite different. On one occasion, an Anglo-Australian kept circling his car parked outside a dance hall and when asked what he was up to, he called Bertelli a 'ding bastard'. Bertelli explained that this was soon sorted out when he:

> bashed him up. After that, that bloke one of me best mates.

At the 'positive' end of the spectrum, Albert Piacentini stated that he enjoyed lasting friendships with Anglo-Australians he came across in the interwar period, some of whom advised him in securing contracts and finding accommodation for his family. His daughter Helen claimed that they treated her father well and were still his 'best friends today'. Both Viskovich and Baruffi were advised by Anglo-Australians to take up citizenship to overcome work restrictions. Baruffi mentioned the Sutton brothers with whom he shared a lasting friendship. Carlo Bertelli enjoyed the respect and friendship of the mill manager at Lyall's mill where he worked. In an incident at the Collie hotel, one of the mill men insulted Bertelli and was overheard by the mill manager who dismissed the offender on the spot, with the explanation that 'he has to learn to talk to people, you see'.

Although Luigi Bertelli was very positive towards Australians and had participated in state cycling competitions representing Collie in the 1950s, he still stated 'I feel I am Italian, no doubt about that'. Aged 97 in 1995, Pietro Baruffi wanted to forget about Italy stating that he was happy to be an Australian. However, the incident at a pub during the depression, when an Australian returned soldier spat in his beer because he did not have the money to buy the Australian a drink, left him stating 'I won't trust an anymore-them person, that's all about it'.

Timber industry turnaround

The turnaround in the timber industry came in 1934 with a substantial improvement in the position of the industry throughout the remainder of the decade. Although hewing operations never again reached the peak of the mid-1920s, they picked up significantly and by the late 1930s between 800 and 900 registered hewers were employed in sleeper cutting throughout the year.

Then, in recognition of the harshness of its fees and to assist in rehabilitating the industry, the Forestry Department allowed a 20% rebate on royalties and a 50% rebate on inspection fees on hewn sleepers from private property.

Having successfully restricted hewing activity on private property, the Department could afford to point to the real culprits of the glut in the hewing trade for export sleepers and the resultant fall in price:

> If it were not for the cut-throat competition of contractors employing foreigners on private property, overseas orders for sleepers would have been obtained at very much better prices.

With the dispersal of the Italian and Croatian 'army of hewers' brought on by the depression and further assisted by the increase in inspection fees, the Forests Department felt confident it could manage the exploitation of the forests. Italians and Croatians fell once again into obscurity and the Department made no further mention of these timber workers to the end of the decade.

The Depression eases

Unemployment fell from a record 30.3% in 1932 to 5.6% in 1936 and Western Australia mirrored this trend. As a result, the federal government felt that immigration restrictions on southern Europeans could be relaxed. In April 1936, the landing money requirement was reduced to £200 for independent (without guarantors) alien settlers. Sponsorship was extended not only to close dependent relatives but also to adult workers (with guarantors) who could engage in:

trades and occupations in which there was opportunity for their absorption without detriment to Australian workers and were in possession of £50 landing money.

Changes in the Timber Industry

A number of small but significant changes had occurred in the timber industry. Improvement in the timber trade resulted in a number of sawmills resuming cutting operations. As increasing numbers of Italians and Croatians took up naturalisation, they entered previously restricted workplaces so that, by 1935, there were 92 naturalised Italians and Croatians employed in mills out of a total workforce of 1,912.

A second change was brought about with new technology. With the advent of the motor lorry for bush haulage, timber which was previously accessible only to hewers could now be handled more economically. However, it was the development of a number of small portable mills which produced the greatest change to the industry's method of production and to its workforce. These mills could be easily shifted from one location to the next. Able to utilise a much wider range and lower grade of log, the small sleeper sawmills gradually replaced the sleeper hewers. Technology succeeded in eliminating the hewing industry where the Forests Department's efforts had only achieved partial success.

The development of the small portable mill, or 'spot mill' as it was called, was instrumental in allowing Italians and Croatians greater access to milling operations. The increase in the number of small sleeper mills was so rapid that:

> sawmills are frequently erected and working on private property before the Department is aware of their existence ...which may first come under notice owing

to a serious accident.

The omission of any provision requiring spot-mill owners or operators to register their plants before commencing operations may have facilitated the entry of Italians and Croatians into this part of the industry. Small sleeper mills gradually replaced hewing so that, from 1938, the production of hewn timber steadily declined until its final curtailment in 1945 as Figure 3.1 shows.

Figure 3.1: Production of hewn timber and sawn railway sleepers 1919 - 1945

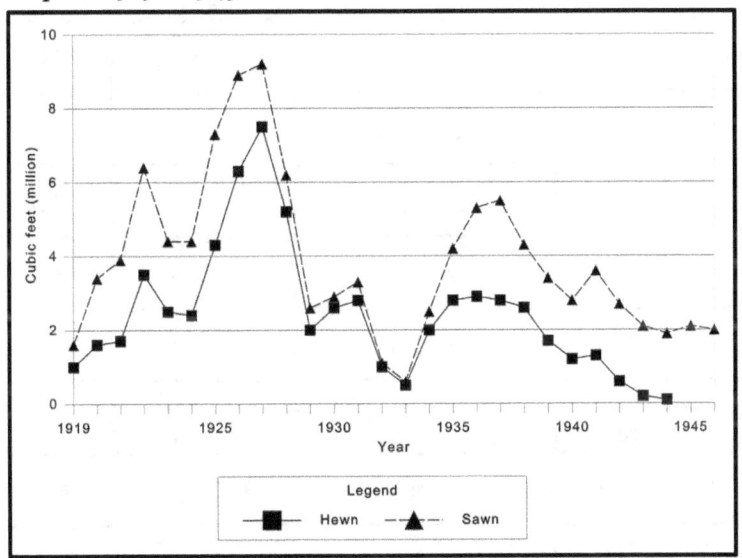

Forests Department Annual Reports 1919-1945

As the number of registered hewers fell correspondingly, these men found employment in the small sawmills. An immigrant presence in ownership of sawmills started to emerge, as Table 3.2 shows.

Table 3.2: Italian and Croatian ownership of Western Australian sawmills

Name of Owner	Situation of Mill by District	Power	Cutting On
Banally, TD	Busselton-Margaret River	Petrol Engine	P.P.
Zorzut & Klanjscek	Bridgetown	Oil Engine	P.P.
Giovannoni, B.	South Bunbury	Oil Engine	P.P.
Tucak, J.C.	Collie	Crude Oil Tractor	P.P.
McCale & Coli	Muja	Crude Oil Tractor	C.L.
Antonovich, G.	Worsley	Oil Engine	P.P.
Tongela, D.	Karragullen	Electric Motor	C.L.
Trevena, E.	Kirup	Oil Engine	P.P.
Zito, G.	Kirup	Steam	P.P.
Sepich & Ruzich	Manjimup	Oil Engine	P.P. & C.L.
Paterson & Zeleste	Mornington	Crude Oil Tractor	P.P.
Antulov, M.	Wuraming	Oil Engine	P.P.
Evanoff & Bozinoff	Wuraming	Oil Engine	P.P.
Lucev Bros	Wuraming	Oil Engine	P.P.

Legend: P.P. = Private Property; C.L. = Crown Land
Forests Department Annual Report 1937

However, aliens were still restricted to those mills

which operated on private property. Vince Nani recalled that:

> Only naturalised people had the right to work in the forestry. The other way had to be private - if the bush is private. If he want to get the timber from the Forestry, you could not employ a bloke in the mill if he was not naturalised.

New arrivals in the late 1930s:

Conditions had not eased for new arrivals. At the Italian Club in Bunbury in 1995, Vince Nani recalled the conditions when he arrived in the south-west town of Harvey with his mother and his sister in 1938 to join his father. Nani described the difficulty of finding steady work:

> a few months, then the work stopped. You stay in Perth or some of the other places to live until you get another job. In 1939, we got this job cutting wood, so much a square metre. And then after a month because we were not naturalised the forestry said "I'm sorry but you can't stop here. You gotta go." because we were not naturalised.

In their interviews, Vince Nani and Cesare Coli stated that hewing was still the main point of entry into the Australian workforce in the late 1930s. Giacomo Palandri returned to Australia in 1936. As he was a naturalised immigrant, Palandri bought a 300 acre uncleared block of land at Margaret River in 1939. As he had done before his return trip to Italy, Palandri bought his own truck and subcontracted sleeper cutting to gangs of cutters.

Perhaps the most optimistic view of this period was put forward by Luigi Bertelli who explained:

me brother left school, and three of us were working in the mill (Lyall's Mill near Collie), see dad was getting nearly £3.10 a week and I was getting £4 a week and me brother was getting £2.10, he started off from scratch. Actually, back in 1936, maybe a bit before that, we were like millionaire, you know, as far as we were concerned.

On-going prejudice

From 1935 to 1938 Italian and Croatian immigration increased sharply. Although immigration officials pointed out that half of the immigrants were wives and children of Italians already settled in Australia, hostility to the presence of Italians and Croatians resurfaced. In August 1937, 89 Anglo-Australians penned a protest to the Commonwealth government regarding 'the influx of large numbers of Southern Europeans into Australia' which they believed was not 'in the best interests of National life of the Commonwealth'. The protesters, fellow travellers with a number of Italians and Croatians on the "Otranto" bound from London to Australia, complained on the 'type of people', commenting that these immigrants were:

> not physically and mentally fit to contribute to the population of our great Commonwealth.

Rumblings of war

The imminent outbreak of war in Europe increased the disquiet about the presence of non-Britishers in Australia and heralded a flurry of activity on all fronts. Authorities grew more aware of the need to monitor alien immigrant movement and activity. The large Yugoslav community in the south-west timber industry drew the attention of authorities, especially as some were ardent members of the Communist Party which was growing in numbers and influence in Australia prior to the outbreak of the second world war. Mate Alac spoke of the severe work restriction he experienced because of his perceived communist activism.

In June 1939, an *Act* for the registration of aliens was passed aimed at establishing better control of their movement and activities. In addition, photographs and certificates of health and character were required of every 'white alien' seeking entry to Australia. The deteriorating situation encouraged many to sponsor their families and, those who could, to obtain naturalisation. Giacomo Palandri sponsored his wife and three children in 1939.

Following the outbreak of war, alien immigration into Australia was severely restricted and in 1940 the admission of aliens from European countries was 'virtually suspended'. Stefania Rijavec remarked how lucky she was to have managed to come to Australia before the war and the closing of migration from her country:

> *son sposata con procura... con suo fratello, perche s'e non sposata, non si poteva venire in Australia. E arrivata... sull'ultimo nave... che son venuta dopo e cominciata la guerra, tutto chiuso. ...sull'ultimo nave. Come sono fortunata!* [I was married by proxy to his brother because if you're not married you could not come to Australia. I came on the last ship. Those who came after the war had started, all closed. ...on the last ship. How lucky I am!].

Giulio Carzoli and Marco Radomiljac both became naturalised around 1939. Giulio Carzoli did so on the advice of his father-in-law who told him that 'they were interning people who weren't naturalised'. Josie Carzoli discovered that, although she was 'an Australian', born in Australia, marriage to an Italian had resulted in the loss of her British citizenship. She was not made aware of this until her husband showed her his naturalisation papers which stated that 'Elsie Josephine Carzoli also becomes naturalised...British subject'. Likewise, Elsie Radomiljac had lost her British nationality when she married her husband in 1935:

> It wasn't till after he got his papers back that they wrote and said that I wasn't naturalised. ...Well I had to get naturalised back ...It cost me 10 shillings to get my British nationality back again.

Despite there being no formal 'disabilities', Italians and Croatians who became Australian citizens did not expect full rights or equal status with Anglo-Australians. They told me in their interviews that they found it 'understandable' not only that there was a hierarchy of preference for employment favouring Anglo-Australians but also that the host society was prejudiced against them. This, coupled with the reinforcement of xenophobic sentiments which became more pronounced with the outbreak of war in Europe in 1939, was to have serious consequences particularly on Italians in the ensuing years.

Loading logs, circa 1937. Left to right Albert Piacentini and Joe Palandri *(photo courtesy Joe Palandri)*

Timber and sleeper cutters around Busselton, circa 1938-39. Left to right Joe Arboit, Nevil Resta, Pino Omodei, Jack Omodei, Jack Marshall and Phil Ryan *(photo courtesy Joe Palandri)*

Survival: Naturalisation and Mobility 75

Sleeper cutters around Busselton, circa 1937. Left to right Jack Valentini, Giacomo Palandri and Giuseppe Tosi *(photo courtesy Joe Palandri)*

Around Busselton, circa 1937. Left to right Giacomo Palandri, Leonilda Palandri and Carlo Palandri *(photo courtesy Joe Palandri)*

4

Aliens of all types: Civil, Friendly and Enemy Aliens

Experiences varied greatly among Italians and Croatians during the war period. After the hardships of the depression years and the shrinking employment opportunities for aliens, wartime restrictions were not enough to dampen the spirits of those immigrants who were at last able to rely on a steady income. Acute labour shortages and the need for increased production to sustain the war effort ensured that Croatians and those Italians who escaped internment could finally be assured continuous employment. 'During the war was not too bad', reflected Basileo Dell'Agostino. Pietro Baruffi echoed these sentiments stating:

> there was plenty job for anybody ...you don't need to worry about that.

Vince Nani had to borrow money to purchase food when war broke out. It was not long, however, before the contractor who had loaned him the money employed him hewing sleepers on private land near Donnybrook.

Nani was overjoyed to receive:

> the first money. You make nearly a pound a day in wages. It was hard work from eight to dark, and from then on, my father and I, we never look back!

Italians were classified as 'enemy aliens' often without consideration of their naturalisation status. Having learnt the lessons of 'visibility' during the depression, they generally sought to keep a low profile to attract as little attention as possible to their presence. At the other end of the scale, those who were interned found their lives cruelly disrupted. Whether as enemy aliens, as civil aliens (that is, enemy aliens and refugees enlisted into the Civil Aliens Corps to address rural demand for labour) or as prisoners of war transported to Australia from Europe and Africa, the war period cemented the labour market presence of Italians, in particular, in the timber industry.

Croatians fared better. Croatia joined the Axis forces and theoretically Croatians should have been included as enemy aliens. However, Australian authorities categorised them as friendly aliens. The 1940s presented opportunities rather than disadvantages to Croatians who became invisible in official records.

Aliens and Enemy aliens

Throughout the period of World War II, aliens and enemy aliens in particular were subjected to the greatest discrimination and loss of liberties. As the largest and most visible non-British group, Italians were targeted where they were not interned. Contemporaneous reports show that they were:

> spontaneously assaulted and their business premises

were vandalised. Boycotts forced many Italian businesses to close permanently and employers dismissed Italian workers to avoid industrial disputes.

As early as 1938, with Europe on the threshold of war, the Federal government set up a Manpower Committee which established a national register to evaluate the Reserved Occupations and for the allocation of manpower. To begin with aliens were not considered a labour resource. This changed from June 1939, when non-naturalised Italians had to obtain written permission before travelling beyond the police district in which they were registered and before changing place of abode. They were prohibited from purchasing or leasing land. In addition, under National Security Regulations, they could be prohibited from having certain possessions which included firearms or related materials, all forms of communication equipment including radios and telephones (or homing pigeons), cameras or other photographic equipment, and all forms of vehicles, including boats. Italian language publications, public assembly and propaganda were strictly forbidden. Those classified as 'harmless' enemy aliens would receive 'sustenance' until they could find employment.

Friendly aliens

'Friendly aliens' such as the Croatians were mostly invisible during the war period. Ivan Surina moved from one bush camp to the next during the war, working for Bunning Bros as a tree faller. Cvitko Ucich worked for the Karri Timber Company at its mill in Nannup when war broke out. He recalled that there were four or five Italians and three 'Yugoslavs' employed at the mill who were ordered by Manpower authorities to remain in this work. Ucich left in 1945 after Manpower restrictions had been lifted. He joined the air force, returning to the timber industry after being discharged later that year. At his home in Harvey in 1995, Ucich recalled that:

> We got treated all right, because I wasn't Italian. The others that were Italians, they had a little bit harder time.

Many Croatians had moved out of the timber industry into other occupations. Giuseppe Rijavec, for example, had:

> *comprato trukko e andato farla legne per King Edward Hospital, portava legne per scaldare hospital.* [bought a truck and went to make wood for King Edward Hospital, he carted wood to heat the hospital]

Marco Radomiljac purchased some land in Middlesex, on the outskirts of Manjimup, and planted an orchard and grew potatoes. He never returned to the timber industry.

Internment

After Italy entered the war on 10 June 1940, Western Australian authorities moved swiftly to take Italians into custody. Those known to have been active in local Fascist organisations or who kept in touch with fascists in Italy and Italian reservists liable to be called for military service in Italy were targeted. About 1,200 Italians were interned from Western Australia and 9% of these were either naturalised British subjects or born in Australia. Some Italians had anticipated that the Australian government would take precautions especially against fascist sympathisers, but many of the 750 taken from rural areas around Harvey and Waroona were shocked at the:

> *interminabile catena di arresti indiscriminati (che) ...causo lo spopolamento e la depressione di quelle aree con il conseguente abbandono delle campagne* [indiscriminate chain of arrests (which) ...caused the depopulation and the depression of those areas with the consequent abandoning of the countryside].

National Security Regulations did not apply to persons born in enemy countries who had become naturalised British subjects. This was often not the case in practice. Under Rule 28 of the *Defence (National Security - Aliens Control) Regulations*, if the Minister of Defence so directed, the orders relating to enemy aliens could also be applied to other aliens or naturalised British subjects. Ethnicity was viewed by authorities as a disability not easily overcome.

The timber industry

At the pre-war planning stage, the Federal government realised that there would be an enormous increase in defence demands for timber. However, despite the inclusion of the timber industry in Western Australia in the list of Reserved Occupations, the Forests Department could not prevent the depletion of forestry department personnel.

Timber production in Western Australia's south-west fell steadily from 1938 due mainly to the outbreak of war and the consequent closure of some export markets for sleepers. Although local demand for timber for war-time use increased from 1939, losses from the ranks of timber workers created a labour shortage which adversely affected output. As a result, an additional clause was included in timber tendering contracts:

> Provided that in the event of British subjects not being available for employment the permit holder may on application in writing to the Conservator of Forests be granted authority to employ unnaturalised men until 31.12.1941 when such authority will be subject to review.

Aliens in the timber industry

Attempts to utilise aliens as a source of labour to replace soldiers were carefully handled so as not to antagonise the Anglo-Australian workforce. Aliens were allowed to participate visibly in the labour market only when it was clear that the labour shortage in the timber industry was at crisis point. Experienced non-naturalised sleeper hewers such as Baruffi and Nani were allowed temporary registration to work in the timber industry where they could finally earn a steady income.

The war brought about a further change in service provision by the Forests Department. Enlistment in the Armed Forces and transfers to other industries had so depleted the ranks of the men in firewood collection that the Perth metropolitan area faced an acute shortage during the winter of 1942. In order to address this, the Commonwealth government declared in February 1942 that all male enemy aliens between 18 and 60 years of age could be directed to civil employment. By the end of the month, this pool of alien labour was allocated to the Forests Department.

The introduction of enemy aliens to the timber industry prompted sawmillers to propose that they also be allowed to employ small numbers of alien labour in timber industry work. At the end of 1942, there were 114 sawmills operating with 2,615 employees, of whom 347

(13.3%) were 'foreign' with Italian and 'Slav' aliens making up 6.5% and 2.3% respectively of the timber industry workforce. In addition, the labour crisis in Western Australia's rural south-west necessitated the pooling of resources between departments. The Forests Department teamed up with the Department of Agriculture to provide men according to seasonal requirements to help with vegetable crops for army consumption. Enemy aliens who had not been interned were employed under the control of Conservator of Forests on potato digging.

The Civil Aliens Corps (CAC)

The Civil Aliens Corps (CAC) was constituted in June 1943 under the Allied Works Council to address ever increasing rural demand for labour. In Western Australia, the Civil Aliens Corps was merely a restructuring of the more informal special labour corps established earlier under the control of the Forests Department.

The Civil Aliens Corps heralded an important shift in the use of alien labour which had become not only politically acceptable but also necessary for two reasons. On the one hand, labour shortages became so acute in 1943 that all available sources of labour had to be utilised. On the other, Anglo-Australians demanded that aliens should also be brought under the same regulations and restrictions that applied to them with one State Member of Parliament complaining that:

> Italians were earning £2 daily there digging potatoes while Australian soldiers were fighting at 6/- a day and this kind of thing was likely to cause a great deal of trouble... If these aliens cannot be used to help the war effort what in the hell are they in this country at all

> for... Some of them are making fortunes out of our misfortunes.

Regulations stipulated that aliens were employed in the Civil Aliens Corps under terms and conditions as determined by the Minister for Labour and National Service. The allotment payable to wives and dependents of aliens employed by the Forests Department was extended to members of the Corps but, other than compensation for accidents, the policy was 'no work, no pay', and there was no provision made if the male breadwinner fell ill.

Whilst it was recognised that some members of the Corps would be resentful at being removed from their normal occupation and assigned work for which they may not have been suited, personnel officers overseeing the Corps were advised that a firm but sympathetic approach was essential to encourage a more positive attitude and appreciation of the work being carried out by the Corps.

Farming

The procedure established at the formation of the Civil Aliens Corps was for a manpower representative either to make aliens who were fit available to the Corps, or to defer their employment if their current occupation was on the reserved list. In Western Australia, many Italians and Croatians had moved to farming when employment opportunities in the timber industry had practically disappeared in the 1930s. However, agricultural work was also a protected industry. To the Forests Department's displeasure, these workers were therefore exempt from transfer to the Civil Aliens Corps. Some Italians and Croatians were very resourceful in negotiating their way around restrictive legislation. For example, several members of the Corps who had been released for various purposes in mid-1943 entered essential occupations without proper authority. No steps could be taken to discipline or re-direct them as:

> replacement is almost impossible as the work which they are doing, in almost every instance, is of a strenuous or objectionable nature.

Celso Gherardi, a naturalised British subject, owned a small business collecting firewood in the Spearwood area. He employed between three and six people depending on demand and his younger brother Benvenuto carted the firewood to the wood yards in Perth. However, when Celso was called up into the army and given two months to organise his affairs, he established a market garden. As a result, the army:

> left him behind ...to produce all vegetables for the army. To supply the army, and he can work on the garden and work on the wood and they supply the cities around Fremantle.

Benvenuto Gherardi was not so lucky. As he had arrived in 1939, he had not resided in Australia long enough to be eligible for naturalisation. In 1942 he was sent to the Civil Aliens Corps camp in Gnangara, near Merredin, for about nine months, after which time he was transferred to Jarrahdale.

Italian assistance

Italians who escaped internment and were in industries considered a protected undertaking were often instrumental in the release of some of the internees.

Giuseppe Coli, a naturalised British subject who owned a timber mill in Darkin, asked for internees to be released to work in his sawmill, telling me:

> we did get a few out. Different ones that we knew, that were good workers.

Establishment of the Civil Aliens Corps (CAC) camps

The first camps for the Civil Aliens Corps in Western Australia, under the jurisdiction of the Allied Works Council, were established at Mundaring Weir, Gnangara, Jarrahdale, North Dandalup and Inglehope. The main activity of the Civil Aliens Corps was the maintenance of firewood supplies. From time to time, its members were also directed to other urgent works. Gangs of aliens were directed to build bush tramlines and to supply logs at some large mills cutting timber for essential defence contracts.

Sam Marocchi arrived in Western Australia in the late 1930s. Within two years of arrival, he found himself in the Rottnest internment camp. He was transferred first to Kalgoorlie then to Loveday, South Australia before ending up in the Civil Aliens Corps in Jarrahdale in 1943. Many aliens prospecting in the goldfields or employed in the mining industry were transferred to the south-west to supplement the ranks of the Civil Aliens Corps. Others, such as Placido Bordin, had been directed to the timber industry by Manpower prior to the establishment of the Corps. Bordin was interned at Rottnest in 1940. When he was released six months later, he was directed to work for a firewood contractor by the name of Jack Tomich and he spent the war period cutting firewood near Karrakatta and at Jarrahdale.

War Cabinet: Change of direction

In July 1943, the War Cabinet issued a general direction that:

> for all purposes of priority the production of essential foods (was) ...to be regarded as a war activity.

The Federal Government reconsidered its commitment to building up the armed forces. It declared that Australia's role in the war effort was to provide a base for operations and to supply goods and services. To this end, Cabinet decided to allocate 15,000 men out of the 40,000 to be released from the army and munitions work so that the pool of seasonal farm workers would be increased.

In Western Australia, where rural labour shortage was most severe, reciprocal arrangements for labour resources between the Forests Department and the Department of Agriculture had been in place since early 1942. These farm workers were now supplied from the ranks of the Civil Aliens Corps, although the men were grudgingly conceded by the Forests Department only for 'urgent' rural work. This rural workforce, composed primarily of Italian enemy aliens, was later complemented by prisoners of war. The Corps members were also called upon twice a year to assist in the digging of potato crops, working from Cookernup to Kirup, Lowden and Dardanup from 1942 to 1944. The Civil Aliens Corps consisted of approximately 200 members and reached a maximum of 260 men in 1944.

Vince Nani was cutting sleepers for Bunning Bros and had twenty acres of potatoes under cultivation by 1943. This did not stop authorities from directing him to chop firewood at North Dandalup in between planting and harvesting. In return, some 40-50 members of the Civil Aliens Corps were sent to his and to other farms in the Donnybrook-Benger area, 'when the *patate* [potatoes] was ready to pick'.

Discipline and Protest

Many aliens complained of not being physically fit enough to work in the timber industry or in forestry work and often failed to turn up when ordered to return to work. Others protested at being 'treated like slaves'. Such was the dissatisfaction among aliens that most camp superintendents experienced problems maintaining discipline especially with regard to aliens who went away from camp without leave. Many aliens turned up when it suited them rather than when told to do so.

Aliens were allowed three days' leave per month. However, Gherardi recalled that during busy periods, leave was postponed. Contravention of the above regulations rendered the member of the Corps liable to a reprimand, cancellation of leave, suspension without pay, a fine not exceeding £2 or, alternatively, the offending member could be brought before a Court and face a fine of up to £100 and/or a maximum six months imprisonment if convicted. According to Giuseppe D'Attilo:

> the law was very strict, we had to be good workers and do more than our best to keep the bosses happy ...some of the boys who could not pull their weight were put in jail.

Discipline and conduct of aliens employed in the Civil Aliens Corps generally did not present problems, yet forester J. Giblett, located at Benger in 1942 and then at Jarrahdale, seemed to 'strike continuous trouble with the men under his control'. Many of the men in the Civil Aliens Corps such as Antonio Paparone were non-naturalised Italians who had escaped internment. Paparone worked as a waiter in Fremantle when he was called into the Corps. After a medical examination, he was directed to Benger to cut wood and dig potatoes. He recalled his lack of preparedness for conditions at Benger:

> was tents all over the place. But there was no bed, nothing. They told me to take the plates, forks and knives, cutlery ...and the blankets. They give you four sticks to make up a bed. I didn't know how to make a bed, but I had to do it. Mattress was a chaff bag, that's all.

The men at Benger were especially resentful of the way forester Giblett treated them. At his home in Fremantle, where Paparone lived in retirement in 1996, he could not keep the bitterness out of his voice:

> the government give us everything. You couldn't wish for better... But, Mr. Giblett, he was a good man, you know. When he used to get the meat, he used to hang em outside for a couple of hours... when it was a good day, you got sunshine. You'd be surprised how many flies would be hanging on that. And then he used to give it to us. I don't think he had a heart!

One week, Paparone and two friends absconded to Fremantle for a few days to catch up with their families. They returned to the farm in Benger where they had been digging potatoes and, before long, three policemen came to question them. Paparone reflected, 'we were young and we home sick'. As a result their leave permits were cancelled for two months.

In May 1943, a few Italians at Benger camp, allegedly 'under the influence of intoxicants', addressed some abusive remarks at forester Giblett who called in the police. All four ringleaders were arrested. Paparone and most of the Italians at Benger were transferred to Jarrahdale with Giblett who continued to be a difficult camp supervisor. Paparone believed that he took pleasure in insulting the Italians:

> I went and see him one day and said we run out of butter. Oh, he said, you got plenty of grease in the kitchen, plenty fat in the kitchen. That's what he said... that's what made life difficult.

To an 'old hand' such as Benvenuto Gherardi, camp conditions were not bothersome. As a firewood collector he was used to camping in the bush. Retired and living at his home in Spearwood in 1996, Gherardi described the washing facilities at Jarrahdale:

> Shower... we had to go in the creek. To have a shower, sort of a bucket, a copper boiling in the kitchen for warm water in the winter time. A bucket... you hook it up sort of, in the open air it's better see, the steam won't affect anybody. And they put a string on your toe. And when you want the water, use your toe and the water come down on you, see. If you lift it up too much, you don't have water (to) finish to wash yourself. You have to be careful.

Gherardi seems to have been an exception. Although D'Attilo had lived in the bush in tents, he described the Jarrahdale camp as 'miserable'.

Conditions proved intolerable for those unused to

Aliens of all types: Civil, Enemy and Friendly Aliens 91

bush living and to wood cutting. It was not long before the men at this camp, directed to cut and handle firewood, organised a 'sit down' and 'hunger strike' in April 1943. The men refused to work unless provided with better living and work conditions. The strike made its way into the press and elicited a strong response from the D.C. Gardyne, Controller of Aliens at the Allied Works Council. Gardyne labelled the demands of the protesting men as extraordinary given that aliens possessed no right to strike. He condemned the lack of swift disciplinary action which allowed the strike to proceed and to be publicised, stating that prompt action should have been taken to prosecute those who refused to work. However, Gardyne noted that:

> It does appear from the many complaints raised that there may be some grounds for genuine complaint. I have in mind that there have been repeated troubles at the Jarrahdale camp, and I wonder if the man in charge is handling the men in the right manner.

As unauthorised leave from campsites had been one of the main issues of concern, Gardyne pointed out that leave from camp had to be seen by members of the Corps as 'a privilege and not a right'. None of the men was charged as a result of the strike but, in December 1943, several men including the ringleaders were transferred to another camp in Alice Springs.

The war took a new turn when Italy surrendered in 1943. However, not much changed for Italians in Australia as will be seen in the following chapter.

5

Italy surrenders: ex-Internees and Prisoners-of-War

Italy surrendered on 8 September 1943 and, having negotiated a separate armistice with the Allies, declared war against Germany. However, the official position with regard to Italian nationals was that:

> With the termination of hostilities it does not imply that Italy ceases to be an enemy country. The formal state of War continues until the signature of a final Peace Treaty. All Administrative War measures taken on the entry of Italy into the War should, therefore, remain in force pending instructions to the contrary.

The provisions of the National Security (Aliens Service) Regulations regarding Italians serving in or liable to serve in the Civil Aliens Corps remained unaltered. By the end of the year, 150 internees released from South Australia were dispatched to Western Australia to work in forestry under the direction of the Deputy Conservator of Forests.

Unrest and protest

The disastrous consequences of internment for both those separated from their families and those left behind often to cope with young children and farms caused much anger and resentment. Wives and families of internees were eligible for assistance at the same rate as applied to families who came under the Child Welfare Department. However, many were unaware of its availability. Maria Bordin applied for assistance for herself and their three-year-old son when her husband was interned, but was refused on the grounds that she was young and could find work.

When some of the interned men were released into the ranks of the Civil Aliens Corps in Western Australia from 1943, they were often an 'unwilling body of workers', distrustful of authorities, disrespectful of the rules, and difficult to direct. Among the men assigned to Jarrahdale were Sam Marocchi and Angelo Marchesi. Both men were distressed by the lack of facilities at Jarrahdale which fell far short of those they had enjoyed at Loveday Camp in South Australia. Retired and living at his home in Perth in 1996, Marchesi recalled the camp conditions at Jarrahdale:

> *Non c'era higene. Non c'era acqua. L'acqua era quella che passava giu nel ruscello che passava... Era freddo - freddo come quella del fridge. ...il cibo, lasciava desiderare.* [There was no hygiene. There was no water. The water was that which flowed down there in the nearby stream... it was cold - cold as that water out of the fridge. ...the food, it left much to be desired].

Within a month of their arrival in Western Australia, unrest broke out at Inglehope and Jarrahdale. The ex-internees had been advised, prior to their departure from

Loveday, that they would be engaged to cut wood and were to receive £4.16.0 per week as remuneration. Whilst this was the rate applicable to members of the Civil Aliens Corps, a system of payment by results applied when members of the Corps were assigned to work in firewood production and potato digging. Marchesi recalled how they were dropped off into an area of bush from eight in the morning until five. They chopped wood all day and stacked it into 'cords'. Piece rates applied according to the number of cords they produced. Whilst the 'old hands' could earn up to £6 or £7, newcomers to the industry like Marocchi had to work hard to earn £4. The men at Inglehope and Jarrahdale, most of whom could not speak or understand English well, believed that they had been misled by the authorities. One of their spokesmen at Inglehope, Francesco Viola, protested that 'it's slavery ...and we are not going to do piece work'. According to Maria Bordin:

> they'd been away all these years... They had earned no money. And they were looking forward to earning a bit of money. But instead they were only paid so much. So therefore there was a bit of trouble.

Trouble also erupted with ex-internees who were assigned road work on wages. In 1996, Sam Marocchi recalled that:

> We used to get £4 a week, but then we had to pay tax, so much for the tent, so much for the groceries, so we finished up with just about nothing.

In Giuseppe D'Attilo's view:

> We can't talk about wages because we got very very little, even though we were classified as soldiers

without uniform we had to pay for all our needs e.g. boots, clothes, blankets.

An incident with a water drum some two months after arrival resulted in Marocchi being transferred to wood cutting on piece rates. The men allocated to road repairs often worked far from the camp site and from the availability of fresh water. It was customary in these circumstances for forester Giblett to supply the men with a drum of water for drinking. According to Marocchi:

> He sent this drum, rusty... How can we drink rusty water with that oily stuff at the top?

Unfortunately Angelo Marchesi drank the water:

> *Era un drum di quelli arruginiti. E invece di cambiare l'acqua, invece di cambiarla tutti giorni... e ho bevuto e m'ha fatto mal di pancha. Allora la mattina dopo che sono andato li, ho buccato il drum, e ho buttato fuori nel bosco. Loro allora mi hanno preso a ripicco. Mi (hanno costringiato)... a far queste cose!* [It one of those rusty drums. And instead of changing the water, instead of changing it every day... and I drank it, and it gave me a stomach ache. So the next morning after I had been there, I punched a hole in the drum, and I threw it away into the bush. Well they had piqued me. They (made) me do these things!]

Marchesi was called up the next morning and questioned. He spoke out against their treatment in the Jarrahdale camp, stating:

> *voi altri non avete diritto di trattarsi noi cosi* [you have no right to treat us like this].

The result was that he was put on to a train the next day and sent to Alice Springs, thus ending two months at Jarrahdale. However, the incident sparked a protest among the Jarrahdale camp members working on road repairs. Marocchi recalled how they told Giblett 'no more work' and were immediately assigned piece work chopping wood where they were paid according to the amount of cords of wood they produced.

The Forests Department, still smarting from its handling of the strike by aliens, moved swiftly to prosecute those aliens identified as ringleaders of protests. There were three arrests at Inglehope and five at Jarrahdale. Fausto Alessandrini and David Desotti ended up at Barton's Mill prison for three months after which they were also transferred to the Northern Territory. However, another fifty men refused to be intimidated by prosecution. When informed of the situation, D.C. Gardyne, Controller of Aliens, decided to 'relieve' the Forests Department of the (ex-internee) trouble makers and transfer the sixty men to the Northern Territory as he feared they would have a bad effect upon members of the Civil Aliens Corps already employed in Western Australia. This had the desired effect of motivating the Forests Department to address protests among Corps members, because within a matter of days the Department reported that the matter was in hand. This suggests that the cause of the problem may well have been 'over-zealous' forestry officials. In fact, standard procedures for the establishment and control of the Civil Aliens Corps recognised that success would depend on the employing authorities having a clear understanding of the right attitude to adopt:

> Men who have been resident in Australia for many years, some of whom have married Australians, and

although legally they are aliens, have definitely acquired an Australian outlook ...and the attitude of those in charge must be guided accordingly. It is considered that the majority of members ...can be influenced by a firm but fair control to "pull their weight" and develop the right spirit of Corps membership.

Further unrest erupted in November 1943, at the Jarrahdale Hotel. Fights broke out between some 20 Italians, most of whom were ex-internees, and local 'Britishers', and the hotel was closed down for several hours awaiting the arrival of the police. Only three of the Italians had been granted leave to go to Jarrahdale, the rest having left the camp without permission.

The Jarrahdale camp report on the incident described the ex-internees who had been involved in the Jarrahdale Hotel brawl as sympathisers of fascism and 'a hostile crowd towards Australians'. Sam Marocchi's version of events is significantly different. In his opinion, the whole affair 'was a farce!' According to Marocchi, the locals were upset that the Italians were drinking their beer ration and, on discovering that the Italians had come from South Australia, they lost their temper as they 'would not let bloody South Australians drink their rations'. Marocchi recalled that this was a weekly occurrence.

Trouble broke out when two Italians decided to go to Perth one Monday morning without telling Giblett. After walking the five miles from Jarrahdale camp into town, they went into the hotel for 'a beer or two'. They were spotted by one of the truck drivers from Jarrahdale mill who reported them to the twelve men at the mill site. The men went down to the pub to safeguard their beer ration. One of the Italians was a 'strong bloke', so it was no surprise that:

> Many people ended up in hospital because it was quite a fight but apart from that it was funny because there we were, supposed to be enemy internees, yet they were prepared to fight us because they thought we were South Australians after their beer.

The Forests Department solution to the dispute was to refuse permission to aliens requesting to leave camp on Saturdays. The department also ordered some 35 men to another camp in Alice Springs, 22 of whom decided not to go and absconded. Marocchi was one of these men and he spent the next eighteen months working around Perth and the south-west doing odd labouring jobs, mostly on farms. When the law finally caught up with him, he was lucky to escape with a small fine.

Complaints to the Consul for Switzerland

The Italian ex-internees at the Jarrahdale camp were far from happy with conditions under the control of the Forests Department. Vincenzo Marai, one of the spokesmen at the camp, complained to the Consul for Switzerland who looked after Italian interests during the war period. In December 1943, J.A. Pietzker, Consul for Switzerland, organised a visit to the Jarrahdale camp. Marai complained about piece rates and pointed out that:

> the camp was not fit to live in as it lacked all the amenities they had enjoyed whilst still civilian internees at Loveday Internment Camp in South Australia.

On being made aware of the complaints, the Consul

immediately notified Marai that the Italians had to carry out the orders for work given them by the Forests Department under National Security Regulations. He pointed out that these regulations applied to any civilian. About 50 men still refused to work despite threats of prosecution. The Forests Department, through the Allied Works Council, called upon the Consul to urge the men to co-operate. Pietzker advised the men to start work immediately, informing them that disobedience was 'punishable with detention or fine or both'. The Swiss Consul was also asked to intervene on behalf of G. Di Ninno and ten other Italians who were imprisoned in December 1943 for refusing to work under piece-rate conditions. The Consul reassured the men at Jarrahdale that they were not called upon to do any more than other Australian citizens, cautioning them to return to work as instructed after they served their sentence.

On his return to Perth after the inspection, however, the Consul called at the Allied Works Council and pointed out that the Camp:

> in its present state, was not fit to serve as accommodation for the enemy aliens in question.

He reported that 'a great many improvements' were necessary before conditions at Jarrahdale camp were brought to the same level as those provided at the internment camps. The men lived in tents and there was no provision of a heated area for the cold winter months nor were there any means for the men to dry their soaked clothing upon return from work. Existing facilities such as the kitchen were very unhygienic, and the mess hall was open to the elements. The kitchen crew at Jarrahdale explained that, whilst there was constant grumbling, the men 'did not dare to "kick" too much'. The Swiss Consul reserved his harshest criticism at the lack of sanitary provisions:

> the keenest disability is the total absence of any kind of sanitary arrangements and one wonders whether the Camp has ever been inspected by the Health Authorities of Western Australia. To think that the men have to resort to the wide bush for such a purpose and have to wash themselves in a nearby creek, as well as doing their laundering in that same place, is to be forced to the admission that such conditions cannot be described as other than shameful. It is surprising that the men of the Camp have not revolted against these deplorable conditions, and (I have) ...come to the conclusion that they have lost all spirit and courage to ask for at least certain amenities.

He claimed that the men at Jarrahdale could not:

> be placed higher than domestic animals, as far as their living conditions (were) ...concerned.

In response, the Allied Works Council undertook to implement a number of improvements as soon as the men went back to work on piece rates. The Council also promised that proper sleeping huts would be provided in the Camp and sanitary facilities would immediately be erected.

In April 1944, the Consul made a second tour of inspection of prisoner of war camps and included a visit to the Jarrahdale camp on his trip. It was noted that, whilst the men had returned to work on piece rates and were working productively, many earning up to £6.0.0 per week, none of the promises to improve facilities had been met. The Consul reported that the camp at Jarrahdale was in an even more unsatisfactory state than it was on his previous visit.

Breaches of camp rules

Breaches of camp rules continued to plague camp officials, especially at Jarrahdale under the command of Forester Giblett. Divisional forest officers, who were entrusted with issuing leave passes, consistently warned Corps members that a pass was required for leave from camps and that failure to take out a pass or to return on time would bring summary action against them. According to Sam Marocchi, he and other Corps members did not bother applying for permits because 'we know that we couldn't get it'. Marocchi would jump on to his push bike and go into town:

> to buy some stuff to eat, because the groceries they used to give us was not enough for me.

Authorities were at a loss as to how to discipline the men effectively. Prosecutions often did not act as a deterrent. All the Italians interviewed who had been at Jarrahdale stated that most of the time the breaches of camp rules were minor. They mostly related to Italians who used to go to the hotel in Jarrahdale and then stop for a meal with one of the Italian families living in the area:

> There was Mrs Giannatti. She was a widow with four children I think. She used to cook for us. We used to go past, before going to the pub, and said "Get our dinner ready for twelve o'clock". So she'll get our dinner ready. In an hour's time we went to the pub and then back for dinner, see. That's the trouble. Where all the trouble start.

Whilst Sam Marocchi, B Gerardi and others used to pay

Mrs Giannatti for their meals, most Italian families extended their hospitality to the Italians at the Jarrahdale Civil Aliens Corps camp. For example, on weekends Maria Bordin often cooked meals for several Italian ex-internees such as Fausto Alessandrini and David (Ginger) Desotti who were good friends of her husband.

Many of the Italians interviewed told me that they believed that the treatment of Italians in particular was unreasonable. They complained that they were used as a rural workforce in times of need, exploited by the Forests Department in the method of payment and expected to tolerate terrible living conditions. Many stated that the disregard for camp rules was brought on by feelings of anger and bitterness. Incomprehension at the treatment meted out to them resulted in lack of trust and respect for Australian authorities and ultimately for their rules, particularly with regard to leaving camp without permits.

Italian Prisoners of war (POWs)

In response to the ongoing Manpower crisis, the Federal government initiated an immigration programme for the utilisation of Italian prisoners of war as an ideal source of labour for rural Australia. During 1943 and 1944, about 12,000 Italian prisoners of war were imported mainly from India for work in rural industries. In Western Australia, the Forests Department was provided with men from two camps for the supply of firewood. The first prisoners of war camp was established in mid-1943 in Marrinup. This camp accommodated some 77 Italians between August 1943 and April 1946. A second Italian prisoners of war camp was established near Jarrahdale in October 1944 and accommodated up to 150 POWs.

Saverio Bruzzese was one of the Italian prisoners of war who found themselves at this site. He was captured in Africa, and then transported to India with many other POWs before being directed to Australia. Bruzzese spent one year collecting firewood for the Forests Department. He was then posted to Marrinup camp for a few months, working on farms in the area before being moved again to Northam, again to work on farms. Bruzzese reflected that he was well treated whilst a prisoner of war. Even though the work was hard, he enjoyed good relations with many of those for whom he worked.

According to V. Nani, some prisoners of war were employed by Italian farmers who used to look after them well. He recalled how one farmer would drive the POWs on his farm to the hotel and, as they were not allowed inside, the farmer would buy the beer to take to the POWs waiting in the horse and cart outside the hotel. Vince Paternostro, a prisoner of war stationed at Marrinup, stated that at this camp he was sent out to work on farms or to collect firewood.

Mobile workforce

By 1944, 65% of the metropolitan firewood supply was produced by the Civil Aliens Corps. Men were readily transferred between camps and when work in one area was completed, the camps were closed down as others were established. Ben Gherardi was transferred from Jarrahdale to Karnup and then to North Dandalup where he was employed in digging potatoes and carting firewood. In the summer months, he was sent to Gleneagles, near Armadale, as part of a fire fighting team and worked as far south as Collie. He was still at North

Dandalup, then under Forester Crockenberg, when the war came to an end. Gherardi was part of a six men team made up equally of Australians and Italians. He stated that relations were very friendly and this made life easier.

The Forests Department tightly controlled the work that members of the Civil Aliens Corps performed and was loathe to loan or release them to other industries. Perhaps the best example of the Forests Department's tight grasp on alien labour was the application by Mrs Lopresti to release N. Foppoli to work for her running a wood-cutting and carting business. Lopresti's husband met his death in a circular saw accident in November 1944 leaving Mrs Lopresti with three young children (aged 4½, 3½ and 2½ respectively). However, the Forests Department met this request with disinterest. As F. Jackson, a Commonwealth Meat Inspector who took up her case, argued so persuasively:

> Foppoli is not a specialist with the Forestry Department and if released will be the breadwinner for not only his own family but the widow and children of the late Lopresti. ...At one part of it this Lopresti family were living on eggs and grapes. Surely to God that is not to be tolerated in Australia when the changing over of a woodcutter from Pemberton to Jandakot would do away with this condition of living. ...The laws of the land and the law of nature demand that this woman and her children be provided for, yet the Powers that be have shut their eyes and ears to this woman's requirements in the past five months.

Records show that Foppoli was transferred to the Gnangara camp in April 1945, and it is presumed that, based on the promise of assistance from Manpower, another man was released to work for Mrs Lopresti.

Manpower direction had ensured that a number of naturalised Italians and Croatians still worked in timber mills and on timber holdings whilst also growing vegetables on their farms. Gulio Carzoli, Giacomo Palandri and his son Giuseppe, Giuseppe Coli and Albert Piacentini were all instructed by Manpower to remain in the respective timber mills where they had been working when war broke out. Several Italians and Croatians moved into farming for the duration of the war period, and others never returned to the timber industry. Basileo Dell'Agostino had purchased a farm in the early years of the depression and was directed by Manpower to grow potatoes 'for the army'. Like many other Italian farmers, Dell'Agostino generally kept a low profile. He often acted as translator for some of the prisoners of war working on nearby farms. Luckily for Dell'Agostino, he was on good terms with the local police sergeant at Donnybrook, because:

> this young people, they used to play this gramophone, and this woman... she hearin it, she thought we was happy because, about this war... Italy, Mussolini... she put a report in, for me like. The report come straight to the policeman in Donnybrook, he come up and see me ...was pretty serious.

Dell'Agostino owned a gun which he used for vermin and rabbit control. This was taken from him, but later returned after the intervention of the Donnybrook sergeant. Out on his farm in Balingup, Pietro Baruffi grew vegetables and occasionally carted timber. He thought it best to keep a low profile unlike his neighbour who ended up being interned:

> They have so many blooming party ...because the

whole second world war start. The neighbours they complain to the government.

His neighbour was eventually interned. As for Baruffi, he stated, 'they left me alone'. Others such as Luigi Bertelli moved to farming during the war period. Bertelli returned to the timber industry in 1946 working at Dillon's mill before moving to work for Cullity's Mill. In the Busselton-Margaret River district, the Zani brothers, Golich, Zencich, Palandri and Piacentini operated sleeper mills between 1939 and 1945.

Civil Aliens Corps disbanded

The Civil Aliens Corps was disbanded in June 1945 and the 168 men under the control of the Forests Department became employees of the department under direction from the Manpower Directorate. All ex-enemy aliens, now referred to as 'civil aliens', remained subject to the Aliens Control Regulations. They were still required to obtain travel permits before travelling beyond the police district in which they were registered and to apply to the Aliens Registration Officer before changing residence. However, they now worked under normal industrial conditions applicable to departmental employees. Sam Marocchi, who had absconded from the Jarrahdale camp in late 1943, decided to 'give himself up' in early 1945. He was fined £3.10s and sent back to the Civil Aliens Corps chopping wood at North Dandalup. With the disbandment of this corps, Marocchi moved to Perth where he took up the 'terrazzo' trade.

<><><>

The War's end

Following the war's end in Europe in May 1945, the Forests Department found itself with depleted funds owing to low wartime revenue and a large backlog of works programmes. The war had left in its wake a shortage of plant and equipment for the maintenance and construction of mills and a shortage of experienced forestry and timber personnel. This situation was exacerbated by the huge increase in demand for housing timber and other timber produce, such as fruit cases. In spite of the availability of 'civil aliens' and prisoners of war, skilled labour shortages in the timber industry severely threatened the post-war reconstruction programme. Both the Forests Department and State Saw Mills pinned their hopes on service personnel returning to their previous employment and to retraining those who were physically fit.

Ben Gherardi returned to his previous employment in Spearwood, and established a partnership with his brother, carting firewood from as far as Jarrahdale to Perth. He continued in this occupation well into the post-war period. After being discharged from the air force in 1945, Peter Ucich enquired for work around Perth but nothing was available. He was offered work at Hoffman's mill at Yarloop, where the mill manager greeted him enthusiastically, telling him:

> You're the man I've been waiting for - young and upstanding Australian. ...We want you badly.

Ucich spent the rest of his working life (43 years) at mills in Yarloop except for a short interlude at another mill at Kent River.

By February 1946, although unemployment was

increasing, this was of little benefit to the timber industry as many families refused to resume the heavy labour associated with this industry. In February 1946, the *West Australian* reported that these difficulties had arisen because ex-servicemen had an 'increased ambition for calling of higher occupational status'. This shortage ensured that, as late as August 1946, ex-prisoners of war were retained by the State Saw Mills.

Post-war settlement proposals again focused attention on the utilisation of forest land and on timber production. However, such was the shortage of timber for housing that the department moved to allow a number of mills which had sufficient personnel to exceed their permissible cut in order to ease the position relating to timber for housing.

Demise of the sleeper hewer

The war years also saw the demise of the sleeper hewer who was replaced by the small sleeper mills which were the most economical method of producing sleepers. The total number of mills rose dramatically from 134 in the pre-war period to 250 in 1950. However, production was still less than three-quarters of the output of 14 million in 1938 mainly due to the fact that the new mills were small.

Populate or perish

The acute manpower shortages during the war and the threat of being 'overwhelmed by the yellow hordes' allowed the debate over populating Australia, which had waned during the depression years, to surface once more. Acting Prime Minister Forde argued that a population of 30 million in the next 30 years was required to enable Australia to expand her primary and secondary industry sectors and to maintain rising living standards. He warned that:

> Australia cannot stand still. She must go forward or perish.

Forde reassured Australians that:

> no aliens would be allowed to remain in Australia after the war unless they were likely to make desirable citizens and no prisoner of war would be permitted to remain here after the war ended.

The *Aliens Act* of 1947 was another legislative step to address concerns of Anglo-Australians. Under this Act, all aliens over sixteen years of age had to register their name, occupation and movements. As an added safeguard, this legislation stipulated that aliens needed the written consent of the Minister for Immigration before changing their surnames and aliens were not allowed to purchase or own land. In practice, some prisoners of war obtained an exemption. Saverio Bruzzese, an Italian prisoner of war who spent four years as an escapee, was sent to a prisoners of war camp in Sydney for six months when the authorities caught up with him in late 1948. During that time he wrote to friends in Western Australia and Italy asking for references. As a result, he was allowed to remain in Australia. Within three years he applied for naturalisation, and was accepted. As the eligibility period of stay in Australia for naturalisation was five years, authorities must have included his first years as a prisoner of war.

Mixed sentiments

Bruzzese's early experiences as a prisoner of war in Australia and the granting of permission allowing him to stay in Australia left him feeling positive towards Australians, stating:

> *Io son stato qui e voglio morire qui* [I have lived here and I want to die here].

Bruzzese described himself as a 'naturalised British subject'. At his home in Harvey in 1995, Peter Ucich, who was included in his father's naturalisation papers when he arrived in Australia in 1932 aged thirteen, made a point of stating:

> I am always a naturalised British subject here.

Most of the Italians, however, were bitter about their war experiences. Interviews showed that, classified as 'enemy aliens', they believed it wise to keep a low profile. Maria Bordin, born in Australia of Italian parents, recalled that

> I must have been a British subject ...but then they say, of alien parents.

After marrying an Italian she lost her British subject status and, in her words, 'that is a thing that hurt me deeply'. She was resentful at having to hand over one of her treasured possession, a camera, to her sister because of wartime regulations and disliked intensely the restriction on movement placed on aliens:

> during the war we used to stay at home and never go anywhere. ...I had to have an identification card with everything, the prints, even the thumb, my photo and

> everything. I couldn't go anywhere. I always had to have a pass. One time I wanted to go up to Jarrahdale to a Mr Giannatti that had passed away. They lived across the road from us, and I wanted to go to his funeral. I went to ask for a pass... I wasn't allowed. And that really hurts me because they said I should give them four days' notice and I said, I didn't know that gentleman, my friend, was going to pass away!

Marocchi viewed his internment as unreasonable and this experience left its mark on him, stating:

> I was inside there doing nothing. I said, Look. Some people outside they need labour and we're here doing nothing. Why?

When Vince Nani and his father applied for naturalisation, in 1945, Nani was asked whether he was prepared to renounce his country. His responded:

> of course, you got to say yes because if you say no they take you out of here.

Marchesi told me several times during the interview that it was '*inutile* [useless]' to stir up old memories. His internment had caused severe work disadvantage, and his involvement with the protests at Jarrahdale left him with a feeling of deep hurt:

> *Io non voglio aver piu niente che fare... E. Inutile. Non vorrei ne anche lamentarlo, a dirle la verita. Perche per me e stato un tempo proprio... anche I miei amici... e te, perche te...*[I do not want to have anything more to do... it is useless. I do not even want to regret/complain about it, to tell the truth. Because for me it was a really (bad) time... Even my friends ...and you, why you].

Marchesi was condemned even by fellow Italians for doing what he believed was right. In a period when Italians knew to keep a low profile, he had departed from 'normal practice' by voicing his rights and protesting at the treatment of members of the Civil Aliens Corps at Jarrahdale. Marchesi recognised the unwritten code of the war period:

> La parola era quella. This is war time. War time era tutto chiuso. Le cose storte per me, non mandavano eh! E io non potevo supportarle. [The word was that. This is war time. War time, everything was closed (meaning you had to shut up) Crooked dealings/wrongdoings were not acceptable. And I couldn't tolerate them].

One of my informants, whose war-time experiences he also preferred to forget, told me on tape that he felt 'like an Australian' and that he was 'proud to be here' in Australia. He also expressed the view that he felt he enjoyed the same rights as other Australians and that he was happy to speak out about all his experiences. Yet, no sooner had the interview finished and the tape switched off, this person qualified his comments, adding that Anglo-Australians 'really hated us' and things were 'very bad' during this period. This view was expressed by many at the end of interviews. This antagonism to their presence, which permeated all government immigration and settlement policies and practice of the period, left no doubt that ethnicity other than British was a barrier to equal status. Unfortunately, this legacy formed the basis of post-war migration, especially with regard to the utilisation of Italians and Croatians in the timber industry workforce.

North Dandalup Civil Aliens Corps camp 1945 *(photo courtesy Cheryl Davenport nee Crockenberg)*

Benvenuto Gherardi collecting banksia firewood near Karnup, circa 1948 *(photo courtesy Ben Gherardi)*

Pompeo Paganoni with dragsaw, Karnup, circa 1947 *(photo courtesy Ben Gherardi)*

Marrinup Prisoner of War Camp

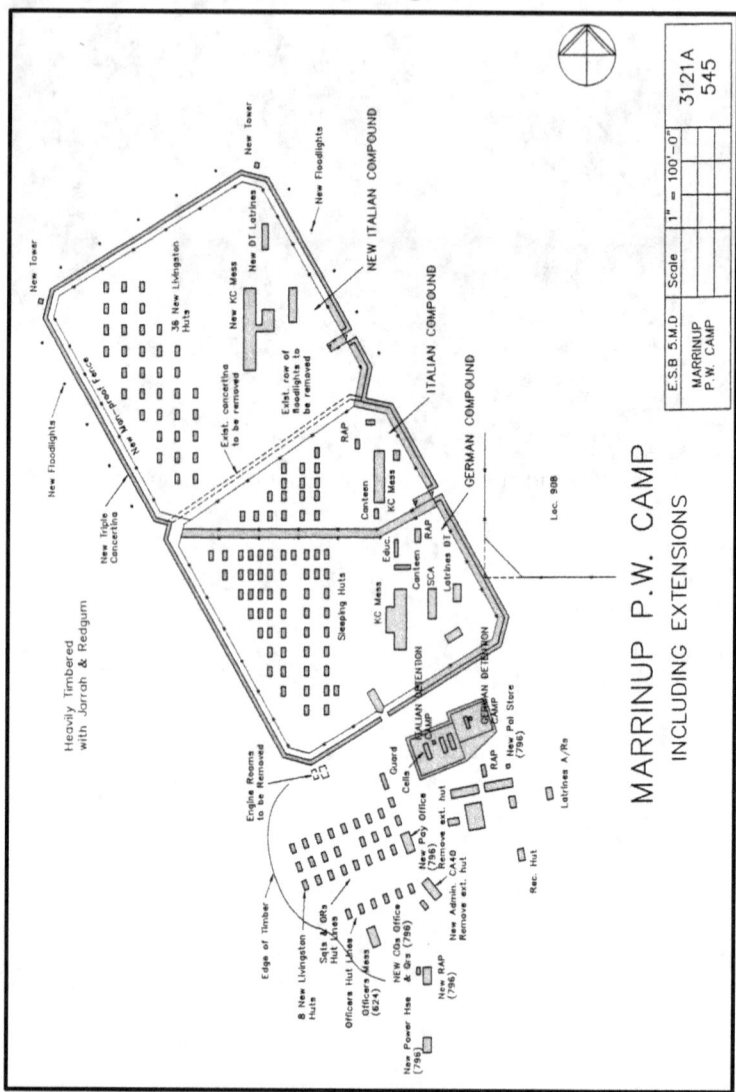

Italians were housed in two separate quarters, Italian compound and new Italian compound. This was due to the different political orientation of prisoners once Italy joined the Allied Forces. Germans were kept apart from all Italians *(Map redrawn courtesy of Marie and Steve Burdett)*

6

Desirable Types

> Aliens are and will continue to be admitted only in such numbers and of such classes that they can be readily assimilated. Every precaution is taken to ensure that they are desirable types.
> Arthur Calwell, *Commonwealth Parliamentary Debates*, 1946.

The post-war immigration programme, the scale of which was unprecedented, has often been presented as a turning point in Australian immigration history. Yet whilst the scope of the programme allowed for an extension of who was acceptable, Italians and Croatians found that there was more continuity than change in their status and treatment.

Australian Citizenship and British Subject status

The aftermath of the Second World War and the focus on populating Australia and nation building reflected a maturation of Australian consciousness. An amendment to the *Nationality Act* in 1946 finally allowed Australian women entering into marriage with Italians or Croatians to retain their British subject status. Then in 1948, the

Nationality and Citizenship Act permitted Australians to describe themselves as Australian citizens instead of British subjects in official documents, yet taking up Australian citizenship also meant acquiring British subject status. Under this Act, an alien was defined as one who was not a British subject.

Post-war immigration

The new federal Liberal government elected to office in December 1949 expanded the immigration intake from 1950. Minister for Immigration Harold Holt made it clear that:

> This is a British community, and we want to keep it a British community living under British standards and by the methods and ideals of British Parliamentary democracy.

Immigration was primarily aimed at attracting British subjects into its fold. As severe labour shortages continued to hamper development, Australia embarked on a broadening of its classification of acceptable immigrants. Immigrants who came from a non-British background were encouraged to abandon their cultural identity and become Australian in outlook and way of life. Under the Displaced Persons (DP) programme, refugees were directed to workplaces under a two year contract. This contractual condition was then extended to assisted passage schemes and the nominee/sponsorship system.

The timber industry

The timber industry in Western Australia, in common with many industries Australia-wide, was severely hampered in its post-war expansion programme because of labour shortage. Timber was essential for the construction of housing to accommodate a greater population, and the shortfall in timber production impeded the state's development. Sawmilling practice in the interwar period had been established upon a vigorous export trade, particularly in sleepers. With housing given such a high priority by the Western Australian government from the late 1940s, the Forests Department imposed a limitation on timber export and encouraged the large mills to switch to producing housing timbers. Then to address the shortage of skilled timber workers, the department turned to immigration. Reassuring Australian workers that immigrants would not displace Australian labour was an important aspect of gaining workers' acceptance of mass immigration. The Federal government emphasised that:

> Migrants (would) be of a suitable type: people to work in the unattractive sectors of the economy.

All sawmilling and timber companies sponsoring Yugoslavs and Italians had to sign an Employment Assurance form certifying that the employment of such labour would not be detrimental to any Australian worker. The term 'New Australian' was coined to encourage their acceptance by the Australian public. In addition, and to counter union opposition, New Australians would work under the same conditions as union members, the difference being in the type of work that was available to these immigrants.

Union vigilance in ensuring compliance was an important factor in dispelling fears that immigrant labour would undermine workers' conditions in the timber industry. New employees who failed to take out union membership were warned that non-compliance would result in their employment being terminated.

Italian and Croatian migration

The availability of shipping from 1948 made it possible for Italians and Croatians to arrive in greater numbers. Right from the start there was a hierarchy of who was acceptable: there were those who were encouraged, those found acceptable and those whose immigration numbers should be limited. Italians fell into all three categories depending on the needs of the Australian immigration programme. Most Italians migrated to Australia in the early 1950s under various nomination schemes where, unlike displaced persons, they were responsible for their own passage costs. In the late 1940s, when the bulk of Croatian migration to Western Australia took place, the majority arrived as refugees from Tito's communist regime under assisted passage (displaced persons) programmes.

As had been the case since before the turn of the century, Italian migration was on a much larger scale than Croatian migration. Whilst no evidence of discrimination emerged to distinguish between Croatian refugees on the basis of their political allegiances, Australian immigration authorities discriminated against the more visible Italians on two levels. On the one hand, those who were known to be fascists or communists were deemed 'undesirable' and denied entry permits to Australia. On the other hand, the 'darker' southern Italians were considered unsuitable and were practically excluded from assisted passage schemes.

<><><>

Croatians and the Displaced Persons Programme

Many of the Croatian arrivals to Western Australia in the period 1948 to 1952 came as Displaced Persons (DPs). Australia first accepted only Latvians, Lithuanians and Estonians - the Balts. Ukrainians and Slovenes were added to the list of acceptable at the end of 1947 with Czechs and Yugoslavs and Poles included from January 1948. When it became obvious that immigration targets from preferred countries of origin were not achievable, the immigration net was cast wider, so that by April 1949 all Europeans were accepted.

The Forests Department and the Sawmillers Association had made strong representations to the Prime Minister to allocate displaced persons to augment timber industry personnel. Between 1948 and 1953 approximately 3,500 'Jugoslav' refugees came to Western Australia under the DP programme, the majority arriving in 1950.

In May 1948, Bunning Bros lodged an application to sponsor ten 'Jugoslav' men who were then in DP camps in Italy. Following the granting of permits for those nominated by Bunning Bros, a substantial number of landing permits were approved for nominees of other timber firms such as Millars Timber and Trading Company Limited. State Saw Mills benefitted from the programme with several displaced persons directed to their mills. As a result, 350 men found themselves in Western Australia's south-west during 1948 and provisions were made for a further 400 to be allocated over 1949-1950 as new mills were constructed.

Tahir Bajrovic and Josip Grguric were two of five Croatians who had stuck together and come to Western Australia under the DP programme in April 1949. They were housed in Graylands before being directed to work in the south-west timber industry. Retired and living at his home in the Perth suburb of Hilton in 1997, Bajrovic recalled that three industries in Western Australia absorbed the displaced persons, namely the coal mines in Collie, the asbestos industry in Wittenoom and the timber industry in the south-west. Both Bajrovic and Grguric were directed to Bunning Bros' timber mill in Nyamup. Whilst at the Graylands camp, Bajrovic had found labouring work at Royal Perth Hospital. However, as Bunning Bros had nominated him for migration, he was advised that he had no option but to go to the mill at Nyamup. If he refused, he would 'be deported back'.

The initial agreement signed by Australia for those immigrants arriving under the DP Scheme bound them to remain in employment found for them for a period of not less than one year. However, the Landing Permits stipulated that foreigners were admitted on the condition that they undertook to remain in an approved occupation for a period of two years. In many cases, DPs such as Bajrovic and his Croatian friends were unaware of any contractual requirements:

> Everybody was surprised. Everybody found out ...when we came in here.... Only when we came in here we know about the contract.

In Grguric's words, when they were presented with a two year contract, they:

> were happy to sign just to get anywhere, start a normal life instead of staying in a camp and not knowing where the next meal is coming from.

Displaced persons were not always allocated work immediately after arrival. Anton Polich arrived under the

DP scheme in 1950 and he spent several months in the Northam refugee camp. Retired and living in the south-west town of Manjimup in 1997, Eva Polich recalled attending English lessons at the camp in Northam. She was bemused by her husband's struggle to grasp the English language. Eva related how her husband had asked for a leg of cheese and was greeted with howls of laughter. After that he refused to attend English classes:

> My husband, that is why he go out of the camp, because he couldn't ...wouldn't learn English. ...And he say, not me, nobody laughs (at) ...me. And he go to the office and ask to be sent out. And they found a job for him in Deanmill.

Living conditions

All major mill sites provided accommodation for married and for single men, but amenities were poor. For the first migrants to arrive at Bunning Bros' Donnelly River Mill, manager Harry Martin quickly erected some rather 'rough shacks'. Bajrovic, Grguric and their Croatian colleagues were transported by 'tray-top' truck from Manjimup to Nyamup Mill where Bunning Bros housed them in their single men's accommodation. According to Grguric:

> It was a little bit of a shock to me. There was this little wooden construction with the wind blowing through the boards that had enough room for two beds, one on each side, and a fireplace in the front. And then in one corner you could have a bit of a table that was our living quarters. There were communal showers. For food, there was a mess hall. It wasn't very pleasant at first. I thought, my God, where have I come?

Eva Polich complained about the initial accommodation

provided by the State Sawmills at Deanmill for herself, her husband and two girls. It was:

> a single men's hut, not nice, only like a shed, and it was fat (dirty) and things ...it was terrible.

Croatians had to contend with isolation which added to their discomfort. In the early years at Nyamup, Ben Bryant described conditions, stating:

> motor cars were very scarce and the road was just an earth road, winding in and out between the trees so that it became quite a chore to go in from the mill to Manjimup and a lot of people just lived their lives at the sawmill. (They) couldn't move away very much.

Wild, appointed Minister for Housing and Forests in September 1950, visited the south-west in October and called for 'a little ingenuity' from sawmill managers. He attributed the difficulty in attracting labour to the south-west sawmills to the lack of amenities at the mill sites and in milling towns. Refuting this criticism, and contradicting the views of Grguric and others, Charles Bunning claimed that amenities at Bunning Bros' Nyamup mill left little to be desired. However, the Minister was not deterred. Wild called for the establishment of clubs in the more isolated centres to complement facilities such as electricity, an adequate water supply, and easier access to schools and to shops.

Dangerous work

Many displaced persons were unskilled in timber work and mill managers were responsible for training the men. Yet training often consisted of 'explaining to them what was safe and what wasn't.' According to Ben

Bryant, they soon learnt what was right and what was wrong and how to look after themselves. Alertness was an imperative both in the bush and in the mills. Not to learn fast could cost a life. An experienced timber worker before he migrated to Australia, Italo Tomasi cautioned:

> Ah, you got to be with the eye on the back of the head. You have to be careful all the time... Too cocky, you put your finger in the bloody saw, you know.

In the four years that Tom Bajrovic spent at Nyamup Mill, there were two fatalities. Bajrovic worked first as a hookman, loading logs for the twin saws and then in the bush pulling logs into the mill by tractor. Both types of work were dangerous. The hookman's job was to hook up the logs, often up to ten metres in circumference, and winch them on to the bench for cutting:

> all logs sit log to the log. When you move the first one, if you not put a block underneath or you no stay on other side, when you move it with the hook... the other ones came behind. So, you have to be smart, you stay out of the way.

After nine months, Bajrovic was sent to work on the tractor hauling logs to replace a Ukrainian who had been killed when the log he was pulling mowed down another tree, a limb of which landed on the tractor:

> When you pulling the logs through the bush, you don't always watch front where you going. You watch behind. Your log maybe go bit on side, it's on a steel rope. It picked up other trees. When I was on that tractor, I was more frightened than in Hungary on the front line against Soviet Union.

Bajrovic was replaced as hookman by a young Italian and within two weeks he was killed when struck by a rebounding log. Yet, despite the dangerous nature of the work and the fact that he hated the bush, Bajrovic stayed for another two years after his two-year DP term was complete because the wages and overtime opportunities were good. Bajrovic was paid £9 a week instead of the £5 he would have been paid working in the mill. In addition, he was paid extra on weekends for cleaning and servicing the tractor. Grguric was employed on road building through the bush for the first nine months. He was reluctant to work in the mill as he enjoyed bush work, but after three months of constant rain or drizzle, wearing clothes and shoes that never seemed to dry out, he changed his mind, stating:

> I finally accepted the manager's offer to work in the mill itself which has got a roof, but also a lot of dust... but it was preferable to the rain and the wet.

He was not so lucky when a log fell off the rollers on the bench and hit his leg, breaking it and severing a vein. Because of persistent pain, Grguric left the mill:

> they let me go because of my accident ...so they didn't complain because I broke my contract. ...I left and went to Fremantle.

Joan Ladhams recalled that many displaced persons were sent to mills:

> into jobs where they shouldn't have been because they didn't understand a word of the language, and our men didn't understand them either, and they were put there and lots of them lost fingers and hands and got injured.

Accident report figures for 1950 showed that, whilst foreigners constituted 14% of the workforce, they sustained 21% of accidents. Without exception, my informants had witnessed several accidents including a number of fatalities so that statements such as 'got killed, poor bugger' were quite common. Apart from the dangerous nature of the work, there were other hazards to working in the mills. One of these was the noisy environment and, with no ear protection, many sawmill employees such as Grbavac and Ciappalone became hard of hearing. Ciappalone told me that timber work was 'really hard ...very heavy and dangerous' work. In fact, the high accident and fatality rates convinced Celisano to look for work elsewhere and he turned to 'digging spuds'.

A good worker

In the early 1950s, displaced persons often made up a third of the workforce in the large sawmills, where they usually worked as bush workers under the supervision of Australian foremen. Bunning Bros' Donnelly River mill, for example, commenced operations in early 1951 'with six key men, all the other workmen being New Australians'. John Scott, who was in charge of construction at this mill, was often entrusted to recruit workers from the Northam camp. At his home in Dalkeith in January 1997, Scott told me:

> We'd advise the camp that we, with Millars and various milling companies, were offering them work, so we were out to choose those we wanted to take. ...I preferred to take people who had come from a rural situation in Europe rather than from the city.

Ben Bryant, manager of Bunning Bros' Nyamup mill chose to recruit Yugoslav displaced persons. In his words:

> As employer of labour for a sawmill, I would be looking at people whom I was sure would give a good day's work and if a Yugoslav came along, I'd know that he would be a good worker. And generally they'd be a stronger race than most. They seemed to prefer work in the forest and so they would get some sort of preference as far as I was concerned.

Peter Radomiljac, himself a forestry worker, believed that he 'was born to work in the bush' and he pointed out that 'Yugoslavs':

> were a very strong race of people. A very strong body... because they came from a very hard country. They can work all day whereas the English people would fold under hard conditions.

Despite these stereotypes, Croatians must have had other ambitions for, as soon as their two-year terms were up, most moved on to other work. This prompted frustrated industry managers to complain that this workforce had proved to be 'not highly satisfactory'. According to Elsie Radomiljac:

> as soon as they saved a bit of money, they all went away... wanted to leave and got jobs that they wanted to do.

Although displaced persons proved to be a transient workforce in the timber industry, migrant labour had been an asset. For example, 'Europeans' had made up 90% of workers at the Donnelly River mill 1950, and the mill's output had risen by 42% from 1945. Whilst the post-war refugee wave of 1947-53 contributed the greatest proportion of Yugoslav immigrants, a few found their way to Australia sponsored by family already here. Jerko Grbavac came to join his father in Perth in 1948 before moving into the timber industry in Manjimup three years later.

The Italians

The Italian community in the south-west was already well established at the start of the post-war period. Italian immigration increased substantially during this time but, unlike the 'Yugoslavs', the vast majority came through sponsorship and not through assisted passage schemes. With the supply of displaced persons coming to an end, Australia and Italy negotiated an immigration agreement in March 1951 in which each party undertook to pay one quarter of the passage costs for selected migrants. Australia was responsible for the initial accommodation, welfare and employment of immigrants under this scheme.

The Australian government had entered into this agreement with misgivings as Italian immigrants were considered to be of an inferior racial type. In 1948, J. B. Chifley, Australian Labor Prime Minister, acknowledged that Italians could be included in the immigration programme. Authorities favoured northern Italian immigrants, believing that 'a bar should remain against Southerners'. Reflecting this view, Western Australian officials wrote that:

> cultural standard, habits and general attitude towards

employment are more developed among Northern Italians.

Although immigration authorities recognised that those who had resided in Western Australia for some time had 'earned good character and business records', it was nevertheless decided that:

> Northern Italians are of a type more likely to be assimilated into the Australian way of life and therefore it would be desirable that the ratio of admissions of Northern and Southern Italians should favour the former.

After a slow start, 9,911 Italians came to Australia under the assisted passage scheme in 1952/3. Although Italians from southern Italy made up the greatest number of migrants, it was practically impossible for southerners to obtain assisted passage. Many Italians who arrived in 1951-52 could not obtain work. They found themselves isolated in camps like Bonegilla where matters came to a head when Italians at this camp rioted in 1952. Vittorio Da Re was thirty seven years of age when he arrived in Fremantle in 1952, leaving his wife and two sons in Treviso, Italy. His two brothers had migrated to Australia in the late 1920s and one of them urged him to try his luck in Australia:

> *Ti faccio venire in Australia per due anni. Dopo due anni o in dietro in Italia o far venir la moglie... Volevo provare come e anche in Australia ...quel periodo che son venuto io, non era tanto facile. Era molto crisi. Hanno fatto il strike per otto mesi I treni in Australia.. Quando dicevano, ma why in Australia, vedi sui giornali, cosa c'e in Australia? Lo so, ma c'ho due fratelli che... sapranno dirmi se devo partire o no.* [I will sponsor you to

Australia for two years. After two years, or (go) back in Italy or bring out the wife.... I wanted to see what it was like in Australia as well ...those days when I arrived it was not so easy. There were many crises. There was an eight month train strike in Australia. When they told me, but why in Australia, look at the newspapers, what is there in Australia? I knew, but I had two brothers here who knew to tell me whether I should depart or not].

According to Da Re, the Australian government had called out many Italians under false pretences, stating:

> the people was on strike and he called the New Australians. Soon we come here, boatloads full.

As a result of the Bonegilla riots, assisted passages to Italians were suspended. This caused much displeasure with the Italian government who believed that the Australian government had acted in bad faith. It was not until December 1954, with the recovery of the Australian economy, that the Assisted Passage Agreement with Italy was resumed and eventually extended to 31 January 1964.

Nomination schemes

Despite mass immigration, labour shortages were still crippling the timber industry. In May 1950, Assistant Minister for Housing G.A. Wild undertook a tour of the south-west mill sites. At the newly completed Quinninup mill, one of the largest mills in the state owned by Millars Timber and Trading, production was at 28% of total capacity, with 34 men employed out of a required total of 160. State Saw Mills experienced a huge turnover in men with 485 men for the required 27 positions passing through their mills in 1951. Ross

McLarty, Premier of Western Australia, on learning that Italians coming in under the assisted passage scheme were being directed to the eastern states, took up the issue with Prime Minister Menzies stating that some seven hundred men were urgently required in the timber industry:

In response to this plea for labour, the Immigration Department advised that firms could recruit foreign workers under a special migration arrangement where nominated migrants were earmarked for a particular company. Several timber companies succeeded in attracting Italian labour to their mills under this scheme. During 1951-53, the Kauri Timber Company sponsored a number of Italians to work as 'Sawmill Hands' at their mills in Northcliffe and Nannup. Coli Sawmills sponsored many Italians with partner D.T. Connell commenting that 'labour for the industry was plentiful if you sent to Italy for it'. Giuseppe Coli went back to Italy in 1956 and again two years later and collected names and addresses of those who would consider emigration and whom he later sponsored.

Both Bunning Bros and Millars' Timber and Trading sponsored a number of Italians in the early 1950s, all of which came from the Sondrio region in northern Italy. Whether they came out as nominees or under the assisted passage scheme, Italians were subject to the same contractual conditions that applied to displaced persons. Corrado Quirici, for example, employed at Millars' Quinninup Mill outside Manjimup wrote to the Immigration Department in May 1952:

> *Io qui sottoscritto ...ingangiato all'avoro (sic.) Tramito dell'ufficio del Commonwealth desidero da voi di essere informato, se pagando il debito del mio viaggio potrebbe essere sganciato dal mio contratto.* [I the undersigned

...engaged under the assisted migrants scheme under the Commonwealth would like to know if I could be released from my contract if I repaid my own passage expenses].

Quirici was advised that he could not be released from the employment contract by repaying the cost of his passage to Australia. In contrast, the timber companies' obligations were less onerous as their obligation to provide work and accommodation was for at least one year from the date of the immigrants' arrival. With the smaller enterprises, however, the two year stipulation was more difficult to enforce. Ben Gherardi and his brother Celso sponsored several Italians to work in their firewood collection and carting firm, stating:

> They write (to) us, if we want to sponsor them, they wanted to come over, see... Some they work for twelve months. And they went off for different jobs. They supposed to stay with people for two years, but sometimes they not pleased. What can you do? ...They always think they better when they get another job, but sometimes it doesn't turn (out) that way.

Chain Migration

A large number of Italians found their way to these shores sponsored by relatives and friends who had arrived in the interwar period. Italian arrivals peaked in 1952 and then again in 1955-56 (Table 6.1). In 1953-4, Italian female migration overtook male migration as those who decided to stay in Australia brought out their wives and families. Vito Pesce, who arrived in 1952, sponsored his wife who arrived ten months later. Similarly Vittorio Da Re brought out his wife and two sons in early 1954, just over a year after his arrival.

Table 6.1: Italian Migration: Western Australia 1949-1956

Year	Arrivals			Departures			Excess of arrivals over departures
	Males	Females	Total	Males	Females	Total	
1949	1,180	431	1,611	16	5	21	1,590
1950	1,086	462	1,548	8	2	10	1,538
1951	1,654	522	2,176	32	1	33	2,143
1952	3,401	742	4,143	128	13	141	4,002
1953	914	988	1,902	210	16	226	1,676
1954	987	1,000	1,987	271	33	304	1,683
1955	2,413	1,068	3,481	239	12	251	3,230
1956	2,299	863	3,162	300	13	313	2,849

Australian Bureau of Statistics

The large sawmilling companies also turned to Italians in their employ to boost immigrant labour. Ben Bryant, manager of Nyamup Mill in the 1940s and 1950s, recalled the informal chain migration links:

> because of the number we had employed, quite often they would come and say, I've got an uncle or I've got a brother or cousin coming out. Can he get work here? ... quite a number of them got their relatives to come out ...and a number of them were able to be employed that way.

Bryant found Italian and Croatian workers to be 'good and stable employees because ...they had an object in life', namely to become established and bring out their families. Joe Celisano was sponsored by his father and arrived in Fremantle in September 1951 to be greeted by his family and relatives. The morning after his arrival he joined his father and brother at Millars' Mornington

Mill, where he was directed to stack wood for the boiler. Cosimo Audino came to Australia in 1952 and went straight to work at Millars' Yarloop mill.

Audino's father, who had migrated two years earlier, had asked a friend to sponsor his son and arranged work for him at the mill:

> So he sponsored me. When I come here, he come to see me. He said, don't do anything foolish or anything wrong, because he was responsible for me. If I do anything wrong, he got into trouble.

Those who sponsored relatives and friends had to ensure that these immigrants would not become a financial burden, because there was 'no dole on them days'.

At both Millars' Yarloop mill and Bunning Bros' Nannup mill, Italians made up almost half of the workforce by the mid-1950s. As with the Displaced Persons, the Italians worked in labouring jobs. Joe Celisano recalled that Italians and Poles predominated in the bush, especially on the railway lines, and in the timber yards, where the timber would be stacked by hand. However, 'inside the mill himself they were more or less Australian'. Guy Ciappalone, for example, did labouring work such as 'stacking timber, cutting fruit case boards and doing general yard work.' Cosimo Audino spent 44 years at Millars' (later Bunning Bros) Yarloop mill, stacking timber by hand. According to Audino, 'you couldn't have any choice. That's all there was.'

Italians were also considered positively by Croatian mill owners. At their mill outside Manjimup, Stefania Rijavec told me her husband preferred to employ Italians to Australians.

Small Mills

The small mill workforce was made up overwhelmingly of Italians, most of whom were sponsored by relatives or friends. They did all types of work and were able to obtain skilled employment and better pay conditions, operating the saws and then loading the timber on to the trucks. Vittorio Da Re, for example, was an experienced timber worker having spent twenty years felling trees, carting logs and hewing and squaring timber for housing in northern Italy. He was sponsored by one of his brothers who owned a small spot mill in Balingup.

Italo Tomasi was also an experienced timber worker from the Treviso region of northern Italy. He disembarked in Fremantle in February 1953 to find that his sponsor had not turned up. During the voyage to Fremantle, he had struck up a friendship with an Italian couple who had been sponsored by a farmer in Greenbushes. Having served with the American army during the war, Tomasi could speak some English and he asked this farmer if there was any work available around Greenbushes. The farmer offered to give Tomasi a ride to try his luck in a nearby sawmill. Aged sixty-six and still a very fit man with no plans of retirement in 1997, Italo Tomasi recalled:

> We left eight o'clock in the morning. We got up there eight o'clock at night... He ring up his friend, he had the mill, he said, oh I got a worker here if you want it. He said, yes, put him there. I coming tomorrow and start work there.
>
> The sawmill belonged to Kauri Timber company. And the boss... the name Herbie Paine - the man is dead now - he come and view me. And when I saw him coming to view me I was scared. Because he was so

black, he come from the bush, and I said, my God ...(if) the boss is black like this, what the worker gonna be!

Tomasi started out felling trees in 1953 for the Kauri Timber mill in Southampton (shire of Balingup). One of three Italians out of a workforce of fifteen, he did mechanical work around the mill, hauled in the logs from the bush by tractor and drove the log truck.

Many Anglo-Australian small sawmill owners encouraged their Italian employees to sponsor relatives and friends. Vito Pesce came to Australia to work for Ted Gamblet at his mill in Bakers' Hill. He was sponsored by one of Gamblet's employees, Louis Biasin, who had brought out many family members during the inter war period. In contrast to many of the post-war immigrants, Pesce had sufficient funds to pay his own fare to Western Australia. Biasin worked as a faller for Gamblet whereas Pesce operated the small bench cutting shorter strips of timber for picket fences. Italo Tomasi brought out some of his cousins to work for the Kauri Timber Company:

> we finished up, one sponsor the other, twenty people from Tarzo, finish up in Manjimup, Greenbushes ...all working on the timber mills.

Kauri Timber Company decided to move the Southampton mill to Rocky Gully, towards Albany, in 1956 due to scarcity of timber. Tomasi spent two weeks there but, as he was about to get married, he wanted to live around Balingup. Frank Jenkins, owner of a spot mill in Balingup, offered him work:

> Because they closed the mill there (in Southampton), several people went there asking for a job, but he didn't want them. He want me, because I was such a handy man. Can do mechanic work, I can do train

driver, tractor driver, truck driver, faller, you name and I would do it.

Italians and Croatians were gradually moving into small mill ownership, but this was to provide yet another clash as will be seen in the next chapter.

On road clearing work, Nyamup 1949. Centre J. Grguric (others unknown) *(photo courtesy J. Grguric)*

Nyamup Mill 1949. Left to right Tadija Grbavac, Josip Facini, Josip Grguric (squatting) and Tahir Bajrovic. *(photo courtesy J. Grguric)*

Outside two-man hut at Nyamup Mill 1950. Left to right J. Facini; T. Bajrovic *(photo courtesy T. Bajrovic)*

T. Bajrovic driving caterpillar tractor at Nyamup 1950 *(photo courtesy T. Bajrovic)*

7

Carving Up the Forest Logging Reserves

From the 1950s, generally buoyant economic conditions and the availability of work made it easier for many Italians and Croatians to achieve economic independence. Whilst many pre-war Italians and Croatians had moved on to the land there was a significant number still working in the timber industry. For example, Carlo Bertelli worked at Lyall's Mill until his retirement in 1961 and his son Luigi Bertelli worked for a number of sawmills around Bunbury.

Many Italian and Croatian farmers were still connected to the timber industry, taking up occasional timber work to augment their incomes. Throughout the early post-war years, Jerko Panzich helped out on his father's farm outside Manjimup, growing potatoes and tobacco and looking after a few cows. Panzich took up occasional work as a faller or clearing land and helping out on other farms in the area. He also spent a year at Deanmill (State Saw Mills) working with the fettling gang, repairing the railway line in the bush. Cosimo Audino summed it up in this manner:

> during the week, work in the mill. Weekend, we used to go out and work elsewhere. Digging spuds, anything. Clearing the lands, whatever you can find. ...It was pretty tough too. If you want to survive ...you gonna work, and you want to put the money away, you got to pay for your fare to come here.

Joe Celisano was fifteen when he started work at Mornington Mill. On weekends he would accompany his father digging and picking potatoes on farms in the area. By Sunday night, he 'was finished'.

Firewood production was another significant industry which attracted its share of sponsored immigrants, mainly Italians. Many metropolitan residents depended on firewood for heating their homes and for cooking. Ben and Celso Gherardi had become established firewood contractors who sponsored many Italians. Vince Nani spent several years cutting wood for contractors before buying his own truck to cart firewood to Perth. He sponsored his cousin in 1951 to help collect firewood:

> I was ..woodcutter and he come and help me because it's no good to go in the bush by yourself... you had to get another helper. ...I was responsible for him, I had to feed him, I signed a declaration.

Others sought to establish their own business. Pietro Baruffi bought a truck and turned to carting timber for the Kauri Timber Company. The company also encouraged him to buy and operate a small mill in Nannup but Baruffi quickly worked out that what he was being paid by Kauri did not make the mill a viable proposition. Giuseppe Palandri was one of the few men left still sleeper cutting in the post-war period. He told me how the axe and saw had generally been replaced by the petrol driven dragsaw and circular saw from the 1940s. Then, during the 1950s, these were gradually replaced by the two man chain saw which was then followed by the light but high powered one man chain saw in the 1960s, so that one faller could perform the work of five to six hand fallers. Palandri did all types of work on his father's farm, in timber mills and clearing land.

A number of smaller mills came into operation during the buoyant local timber trade for housing in the early 1950s. By 1951 some Italians and Croatians such as Giuseppe Rijavec had moved into mill ownership as Table 7.1 shows (13% of sawmills were owned by Italians and Croatians). These mills were mainly small capacity mills and usually operated on private property. Rijavec employed a number of Italians and one Croatian, Jerko Grbavac, who spent two and a half years at this mill working on the twin saws before returning to Croatia in 1953.

The timber mills' tug-of-war

Italian and Croatian timber workers were more heavily concentrated in the smaller sawmills where they could earn better wages. A dispute between these small mills and the larger timber mills over timber reserves, in which the Forests Department played its part, adversely affected the smaller mills. As this in turn impacted on work opportunities for Italians and Croatians, much in the same way as inspection fees had curtailed work opportunities for these groups in the interwar period, developments of this dispute need to be set out.

Table 7.1: Italian and Croatian Mill Owners, 1951

Name of Owner	Location	Name of Owner	Location
General Purpose Mills		Sleeper Mills	
Gerich A. & Co.	Midland Jct.	Coli, G.	Darkan
Grinceri, G. & Co.	Osborne Park	Lucev, T.	Jingalup
Menegola, R.	Albany	Tucak, J. & Sons	Bridgetown
Stanich, P.	Millendon	Giorgi, G.	Cranbrook
Antonovich, J.	Bunbury	Case Mills	
Harris & Del Acqua	Jarrahdale	Gavranich, F.	Capel River
Gasperi, A.	Cardiff	Gibellini Bros	Manjimup
Comparti, R.	Hamilton Hill	Tucak, I.	Bridgetown
Barbarich, M.	Millendon	Lulich, T.	Herne Hill
De Boni, G.	Spearwood	Peruch, J.	Kirup
Lucev, C.	Osborne Park	Brescacin, A.	Kalamunda
Marotti, G.M.	Inglewood	Colobrese, P.	Wanneroo
Martinovich, N.	Osborne Park	Ghilarducci, G.	Kelmscott
Meotti & Foppoli	Argyle	Farcich & Martinovich	Osborne Park
Morellini & Co.	Diamond Tree	Sonego, P.	Kelmscott
Rijavec, J.	Manjimup	Villanova, A. & L.	Wanneroo
Valli, W. & B.	Osborne Park		
Yabuka, T.	Osborne Park		
Piacentini, C.A.	Dardanup		
Manolini & Sons	Yeriminup		
Tucak, J.C.	Dwarda		

Forests Department Annual Report 1952

Despite large scale immigration, timber production - so essential for housing - was still unable to meet demand and this was cause for great concern to the government. Minister for Forests Wild was critical of the sawmillers' efforts and expressed the view that:

timber production, even with the available timber and mills, had dragged far in arrears of all other building materials.

In response to growing complaints about forestry and timber management, State Premier Ross McLarty announced the establishment of a Royal Commission on Forestry and Timber Matters in December 1950. Minister Wild claimed that some of the large timber companies had resisted increasing production because of the price factor. The large sawmills objected to the government's attack on them, especially as they felt that they had cooperated to a large extent with the Forests Department. Under Kessel's guidance, the Department had been very strict with release of crown land which was determined by forest reserves and a sustainable yield.

Royal Commission

In his evidence to the Royal Commission, Charles Bunning complained many small sawmills had sprung up during the building boom and these newcomers into the industry commenced operations on private property with insufficient available timber. They then looked for timber on Crown land and State forest to maintain operations. According to Bunning:

> considerable agitations have been started and outside pressure was being brought to bear on the Forests Department to make timber available.

Bunning felt that it was more important to give greater security of tenure to mills already in operation. Bunning Bros was not averse, however, to setting up small mills owned and run by Italians and Croatians to whom they subcontracted orders. In 1945 Bunning Bros purchased a mill in Bunbury which was handed over to Albert Piacentini. Piacentini shifted the mill to Dardanup and sponsored several Italians to work at his mill. Records show that Bunning Bros paid the registration fees on behalf of some of the small sawmill registered owners such as A. Manolini & Sons, operating at Kojonup.

Large sawmilling firms such as Bunning Bros and Millars sub-contracted lucrative sleeper export orders to small sawmillers. Often they did not pass price rises to their sub-contractors. Unable to get hold of timber permits from the Forests Department, small mills had to accept sub-contract terms and conditions just to maintain operation. Ernie Paine was sub-contracted by Kauri Timber Company to work its spot mill in Southampton. According to Italo Tomasi:

> Paine would pay the men, pay all expenses, pay for the logs and all the timber got to go through the Kauri Timber Company book. And he get paid so much a metre, or a load, them days... and he would do all the dirty work, and they get the good money... We got the expenses, they go and get the log and they get the clean money on the profit they make on the work they giving us.

Other small mills which, because they were unregistered, operated only on private property had a precarious existence, especially as timber from this source was growing scarcer. Vittorio Da Re found it very difficult at times to run a spot mill profitably:

> Quando generalmente Bunnings o la gente cosi mettono sui un mill grande, c'hanno la concessione della foresta. Ci da per trent'anni.... Tutti questi piccole segherie non c'e l'avevano... Non si aveva il permit dalla forestale per I

legname, le piante. Allora si doveva sempre comprar dai privati... Siccome che c'era tante piccole segherie in giro, e tutti privati ...taglia oggi, taglia domani, taglia per anni, finisce ...il privato scarceggia. E allora, sempre piu difficolta. [Usually when Bunnings or others like them built a large mill, they had a forestry concession. It was granted for thirty years. All these little sawmills did not have that. We did not have a forestry permit for the timber, so we had to buy it off private property owners... As there were many small sawmills around, all working on private property, you cut today, you cut tomorrow, you cut for years, it finishes ...private property timber became scarce. And so, always more difficulty].

Giving evidence before the Commission, D.T. Connell, partner in Coli Mills, took up the issue of permits and royalty applicable to sawmills which he felt discriminated against the small operators. Connell stated that the large companies had the benefit of 'virgin bush' in which the permit areas were too big and the royalty payable too low. Whilst smaller mills had the necessary manpower, they were not given a 'fair go' and found it difficult to compete as they had to pay a higher royalty for poor bush. In Connell's view:

> the present system was open to abuse through the big mills getting their heads together and working on the basis of "my turn this time, yours next time".

Jack Antonovich, who owned or partly owned six mills spread over the south-west, claimed that the large sawmilling companies held extensive permit areas at a time when they could not operate to capacity. Speaking through an interpreter in 1951, Antonovich claimed that these mills concentrated on large sizes of timber for export, as these fetched a higher price. He suggested that the Forests Department revoke unused portions of permits and re-distribute these among the small mills. Antonovich argued that this made economic sense since recovery of timber from poor logs was higher in small mills. He suggested that large permit areas should be divided between sawmills and employees could then be housed in a central mill town and transported to work by buses.

The Royal Commission report

The Royal Commission report highlighted the difference of opinions between the new Minister for Forests, H. E. Graham, and the Conservator of Forests, Dr T. N. Stoate, and the tug of war between the smaller sawmill operators and the two large sawmilling companies of Bunning Bros and Millars Timber and Trading Co. It upheld the Conservator of Forests' actions in the allocation of timber permits and supported the reduction of mills which advantaged the longer established large mill owners.

Dr Stoate's position that there was more milling capacity than the forests could support conflicted with Minister Graham's concerns regarding the 'pressing housing demand for timber'. This clash erupted into the press in September 1953 following the withdrawal of the calling of tenders for almost 400,000 acres of land carrying an estimated million loads of timber for sawmilling purposes. A number of the smaller sawmilling companies complained that the conditions of sale made it a cut and dried proposition for the larger sawmillers. For Italians and Croatians who comprised a large percentage of workers in the small mills and who were moving into ownership of these mills this release would have had a negative impact on their work opportunities. They called on the Minister for Forests to intervene and withdraw the tenders.

As a result of this incident, the Minister for Forests established a Forestry Advisory Committee in July 1953 to advise on the allocation and regulation of permit areas and permits and related issues such as royalty determination. The Committee comprised representation from both large and small sawmill owners but it excluded the Forests Department. Several letters to the editor of the *West Australian* pointed out that the committee was heavily weighted in favour of commercial sawmilling interests to the detriment of the Forests Department which was 'custodian' of the forest asset.

In the ensuing debate in the local press, the Forests Department justified the extent of the permit area in the tenders to meet the requirements of the war service land settlement scheme and the needs of existing mills. Harris, chairman of the Forestry Advisory Committee, replaced Stoate as Conservator of Forests in October 1953. Within a year, the *Forests Act* was amended to provide for reappraisal of royalties on renewal of timber permits to remove 'glaring royalty anomalies' that disadvantaged the small mill owners. However, the large sawmilling firms had succeeded in resisting moves to carve up existing permit areas.

Timber production

The acute shortages in timber production for housing were overcome by the middle of the decade. A buoyed Associated Sawmillers and Timber Merchants reported that:

> We are passing through a period of prosperity and expansion as never before experienced in the State,

with corresponding high level in demand for timber. Production of sawn timber is at an all-time peak and the volume of timber retained within the State continues each year to break new records.

This optimism was not shared by the Forests Department which believed that the ever increasing timber output was unsustainable. Timber production doubled from 1946 to 1955. Private property was still a major player in timber production supplying roughly one third of the total timber production from sawmilling. Minister for Forests Graham argued the case of developing private forests so that Western Australia's future timber needs could be assured without resorting to importation of timber. The Forests Department also established further pine plantations as part of its working plans for the provision of the timber requirements for the state (Refer Map 3).

Timber workers: work conditions

John Scott, part of the Bunning Bros management team in the 1950s and 1960s, admitted that timber workers were in 'one of the lowest paid industries in the state'. The Timber Workers' Union pointed to additional factors which acted as a disincentive to Australian workers. These included:

> the arduous nature of the employment, the isolation, the absence of long-service leave in private enterprise and the competitive wage offering of the smaller operators to experienced men reacting against the big operators who paid only award rates.

Union officials refuted claims that a rise in award wages was detrimental to production. Jack Antonovich agreed with the unions, recommending that bush workers should be better paid as they generally received lower wages than their counterparts who worked in town. Many Italians and Croatians told me that they worked hard for little pay. Then as many smaller mills closed down due to a decline in the industry towards the mid-1950s, mill labourers and bush workers faced the prospect of losing their jobs. Jerko Grguric moved to Rijavec's mill because he was 'sick about finding a job all the time'. Cosimo Audino worked at the Yarloop mill:

> they not putting down the wages but they put the men out in the yard. Here, they used to be all single blokes, (but in times of downturn) they used to go working on the railway lines, and all the married people used to work in the mill. At the end, when the job picked up again, we come back working in the yard.

Vittorio Da Re left his brother's sawmill in 1954 because *'le cose non andavano tanto bene* [things were not going so well]'. He went sleeper cutting for eighteen months with his cousin for a small spot mill operating on private property in Manjimup and Yornup. However, the mill manager did not pay them:

> *soldi non abbiamo visto. ...il mill che tagliar il legname per Antonovich tagliava per altri. Antonovich ha dato I soldi... Invece lui le vendeva l'altre parti* [we never saw money. ...the mill which was meant to cut the timber for Antonovich was cutting for others. Antonovich had given the money. Instead he sold the timber to others].

Da Re was fortunate. Antonovich paid him and his cousin what was owed and insisted they take the mill over.

Improving amenities

In the mid 1950s, with chronic labour shortages, many employees were moved to surrounding towns, such as Manjimup, and were transferred to and from the bush by truck or car where this was practicable. In other instances both sawmillers and the Forests Department undertook renovations and improved facilities such as installing septic tanks wherever possible. Bunning Bros gave a glowing report of facilities for their employees at their mill sites in Nyamup, Donnelly River and Tone River which included modern lined houses and huts fitted with electricity for single and married men, social clubs, modern schools, butchers' shops and general stores. Retired and living in the Perth suburb of Dalkeith in 1997, John Scott recalled designing an amenities club for the Donnelly River mill. Scott planned:

> a club where they could have dances, stage shows... where the women can come and have a drink, or the men ...would go into town and buy bottles of cheap wine. If they can have a glass of beer after work, it's far better for them and they'd be ready for work on Monday morning.

Part of the Bunning management team, Scott prided himself that their main concern was employees' wellbeing. Many of the immigrants were Catholics and some of the mill managers arranged for the local priest to go out and celebrate mass, usually fortnightly. According to Scott, this was of particular importance to the women living at the mill sites.

Facilities at some of the smaller mill sites varied considerably. At some mills they often consisted of a basic hut. Residents had to rely on whoever was driving the log truck to bring in groceries and other necessary items and it was a lonely and difficult existence for wives at these locations. Vittorio Da Re worked in his brother's small mill in Balingup after arrival. As this was a spot mill, no accommodation was provided and, according to Da Re, 'non c'erano delle case vacanti [there were no vacant houses]'. He finally found an old cottage on a farm in Balingup which he rented. His wife, Lidia, who joined him after a year, recalled the loneliness:

> was the life there, in the camp, with two children. Only a little cottage, ...very hot weather in January, February, ...and then expect the baby. No electricity, and not the water. Ah, was very bad. I think if I got the money, I go straight back to my town.

They drew water from the dam next to the cottage, which Vittorio humorously referred to as the 'swimming pool', but this made them sick. After two years they moved to another cottage in Greenbushes which:

> non era flash, ma la camera nuova, la cucina nuova... [was not flash, but a new bedroom, a new kitchen...].

At his mill in Manjimup, Rijavec constructed some huts for the men he employed before he did any work to upgrade the old shack that served as a home for his wife and family. According to Stefania Rijavec:

> quel tempi non sono stati tempi come oggi, che potevi trovarla lavorante... Lavorante andavano dove puo mettere sua famiglia [those times were different from today, when you can find workers... Workers go where their families can follow].

When Giacomo Palandri constructed a house for his family on his Margaret River property, his son Giuseppe found it difficult to adjust:

> It took me about a month before I could settle down and have a good sleep. Too quiet and too still, you know, no wind, not any rain in your face, a few drops now and again, I used to love it.

Women in the timber workforce

To the mid 1950s, women did not participate in the workforce of the large sawmilling companies. Bunning Bros' Nyamup mill allowed women into its workforce from around 1955, working mainly on the lighter jobs. According to Bryant, there were only a few women:

> one or two eventually were able to work small saw benches and they became quite efficient benchwomen.

Women were also allowed into the mills at Tone River 'on jobs that they couldn't injure themselves'. According to John Scott, it 'worked wonders' providing opportunities for all members of a family and increasing stability in the workforce. Within the smaller mills, women assisted in all types of work. In the first years after arrival, Vittorio Da Re's wife Lidia and his niece Seconda Da Re helped out for a few days a week stacking timber and putting them into bundles. This did not last long, however, as Vittorio would not pay his wife. Lidia therefore decided to go picking apples instead:

> I not wish nobody go picking apples. Very, very hard work. Ending after ...my back. I got done operation.

In fact all the wives of the timber workers interviewed worked on farms to supplement the family income in the early years of settlement. Farm work was not dangerous, but it was very hard work 'from dawn to dusk'. The women picked fruit, tobacco leaves, and planted or harvested potatoes and most also had to look after children and juggle their working hours with other home duties such as cooking, shopping, washing and cleaning.

Intercultural relations

In the post-war period, there was a strong distinction in inter-ethnic relations between what occurred at work and after hours, at hotels and other public places. The interviews show that relations between Italians and Croatians and Anglo-Australian workers were generally good in the mill sites. According to Tomasi, the reason was that:

> the Italians, they good workers. They couldn't compare with the Italian. With us, at work, because we were working harder, not bludging.

At work, Celisano formed good friendships with some Australians, and he teamed up with Sunny Parks at Donnelly River mill as a timber faller. Retired and living in the south-west town of Harvey in 1997, Celisano recalled

> he was a good bloke... and he teach me a lot about falling because I didn't know much about it.

Celisano added that:

> they see me always as an Italian. For a start you getting upset sometimes. After a while, you just not take any notice.

Most of my informants encountered prejudice in the

towns and in the hotels, stating that name calling was widespread and fighting often broke out between Australians and the newcomers. However, they quickly adapted to the situation:

> for a start you take a bit of attention. Sometimes you didn't know what they were talking about. When you find out the meaning of it you just laugh at it, that's it, because was no good to get into a fight or an argument. Some of them did get into a fight, but in the end of the day, you don't gain anything. So don't worry about it.

Ciappalone recalled that relations between Australians and Italians improved over time:

> they eventually got to treat people fairly decently. It wasn't always the case but they eventually came good.

Vittorio Da Re believed that the great increase in the numbers of Italians, *'tanti venuti, migliaia* [many came, thousands]' made Australians more wary of insulting them or of picking fights. But perhaps the distinction was best summed up by Vince Nani, who believed that, after the war:

> the Australian changed like day and night. Before the war you were a ding. After the war you were New Australian.

Language

Language classes were available for immigrants at most mill sites and milling towns, yet many attended only a few lessons, if any, preferring to learn through 'working with the English people'. The concentration of these groups in labouring jobs resulted in a segregated workforce and made learning English difficult. Celisano, for example, moved out of Mornington Mills after two years because:

> all of this time, I couldn't speak English because they were all Italian on the camp, Italian speaking all the time. The immigrants when they come here, they were not speaking English. Any choice they had was physical work, because they couldn't read, they couldn't write English... so what you do, you go on the shovel, them days.

Bryant recalled that, at the Nyamup mill,

> the Italians and Yugoslavs and other nationalities were very keen to learn English and the English way of living. And so they all pulled together very well indeed.

Language created problems for many. Lidia Da Re found that without English, it was a very lonely existence, 'not understanding nothing, to talk'. She took up a correspondence course in English and complemented this by attending night school in Greenbushes once a week:

> It was the teacher from the primary school in Greenbushes. Every time we reunite there a few people, all Italians. I done a lot one year and then I say, oh I let them down. I not like to learn any more. But and then I got my certificate.

Her husband, Vittorio, reflected:

> A bit hard for us. Still now. I come in Australia to work. To learn another language, you want young people here, not old ones.

Grguric recalled that, although there was a community hall at Nyamup mill, he and his Croatian friends 'were a bit shy in going in because of the language barrier'. Vito Pesce conceded that language problems made mingling with Australians difficult, but he insisted that 'still the people was not impressed to see us here'. Pesce loved dancing and was very disappointed when 'every girl refuse me to dance'.

Children

For some timber industry workers, experiences in Australia commenced at school. Those who arrived at a young age found it 'pretty hard' at school. Joe Celsano 'cried his eyes out' when he found it difficult to socialise and join in a game of football. Domenic Anzellino was called 'all sorts of names' when he first went to school in Yarloop in 1949, aged eight. He left school at fifteen to help out his parents who 'were in a bit of trouble financially' and went milking cows, before entering the timber industry in 1957.

Naturalisation

All Italians and Croatians interviewed became naturalised. Naturalisation in 1952 made 'no difference at all' to Marocchi. He told me:

> I should be equal, the same as the Australians, but they didn't treat us the same. Even in the 50s. But I never depend from anybody. I always work by myself.

Anzellino became naturalised when he turned sixteen, in the hope that as an Australian citizen he would no longer be subject to the name calling which he had found so hurtful. At his home in Yarloop in 1997, he reflected:

> There was a lot of discrimination. I know there was. It was around me. It was put on to me as well. It was everywhere.

Anzellino explained that the opportunity to move into supervisory positions at the mill was almost non-existent except for a few Italians:

> for the ones that had been educated, that were able to read and write and pick up the English language and other things that go with that.

Italians and Croatians who decided to stay in Australia worked long, hard hours and accepted harsh living conditions to achieve their goals of economic independence. However, times were changing. Italians in particular were becoming more aware of their rights, especially after having been lured to Australia with the promise of abundant work. Post-war Italians were more prepared to protest, pack up and return to their homes and for the first time, the Australian government had to turn its attention to retaining this vital workforce.

At Fremantle Wharf 1949. Benvenuto Gherardi (left) and Celco Gherardi (right) welcoming their brother Anselmo *(centre)* who re-emigrated to Australia *(photo courtesy Ben Gherardi)*

Joe Celisano at Benchiasiadale Bush Camp 1959 *(photo courtesy J. Celisano)*

Felling trees at Greenbushes 1962 *(photo courtesy Vittorio Da Re)*

8

Post-war Migration and Competing Interests

> If the need for workers on the timber mills is desperate enough, it might be worthwhile trying to recruit a few families direct from the Refugee Camps in Italy.
> (*Labour Requirements for the W Australian Timber Industry*, Australian Archives)

Acute labour shortages in Western Australia from the mid-1950s particularly in the south-west timber industry provided an important incentive for Australian authorities to slowly come to terms with immigrant disenchantment and address the issue of immigrant work, settlement and status.

Two issues predominated in the post-war period relevant to the ethnic composition of the timber industry workforce. The first was concern over timber supply which was fast diminishing, especially as the yield from private property was expected to 'dry up'. A second factor was severe labour shortages in the sawmilling industry and the focus on continental European immigration, especially Italians and Yugoslavs, to fill the vacuum. Both influences worked in conjunction to facilitate the entry of these immigrants into the labour force of the large sawmilling companies and the Forests Department - the last bastions of resistance to non-British immigrant labour.

'Yugoslav' migration

From the mid-1950s, the flow of Yugoslav immigrants coming to Western Australia increased as many fled the Tito regime. They made their way to Australia from countries like Italy, France and Austria under the Inter-governmental Committee for European Migration arrangements. One such immigrant was Stipe Grubisin who escaped by boat to Italy with his brother and cousin. They made their way to France, where they spent eighteen months whilst papers were processed by the refugee organisation that paid their passages to Australia. They arrived in Fremantle in 1960. Grubisin was fortunate to have an uncle already in Australia who would guarantee them work and their application was processed more quickly than those of other refugees.

Jerko Grbavac had migrated to Australia in 1948 and returned to Croatia in 1953. Disillusioned with life under the Communists, he returned to Australia in 1959 sponsored by Peter Musulin who owned a tobacco farm in Quinninup. He worked there for several months before moving into the timber industry. Martin Panzich, followed by his wife and two sons eighteen months later, also made his way to Australia in 1957 sponsored by his brother Ivan Panzich who owned a farm in Manjimup.

With many Yugoslavs taking up refugee status in Italy, the Department of Immigration established a 'non-Italian national quota' of 500 refugees from Italy in 1956 which was doubled in 1957. Of this quota, 150 persons

Table 8.1: Migration figures for Western Australia for Yugoslavs 1956-1968

Year	Arrivals			Departures			Excess of arrivals over departures
	Males	Females	Total	Males	Females	Total	
1956	154	112	266	8	5	13	253
1957	106	135	241	4	2	6	235
1958	143	95	238	4	4	8	230
1959	114	81	195	17	6	23	172
1960	155	125	280	13	7	20	260
1961	169	134	303	17	2	19	284
1962	190	149	339	17	3	20	319
1963	175	156	331	17	3	20	311
1964	160	113	273	29	8	37	236
1965	166	109	275	16	7	23	252
1966	228	160	388	65	12	77	311
1967	200	110	310	73	19	92	218
1968	267	160	427	92	21	113	314

Australian Bureau of Statistics

were allocated for placement to the Federal Catholic Immigration Committee. Blgica Grbavac told me that she and her family had not come out as refugee via Italy. Rather, the Catholic Church had paid the passage for her and her two sons and daughter. Her husband, Jerko Grbavac, had joined the Communist party in Croatia to be able to get a passport. He told them that he wanted to make some money to bring back with him to Croatia. It was then up to his wife, Blgica, to convince the 'Yugoslav' authorities that:

> He can't stay making money by himself there. I have to go and help him to make money. Then we come back. Then they give me passport ...and when you get it you

run as fast as you can. And when I come here he was happy. He was worried about me.

It took Jerko over two years to pay back the passage fares to the Catholic Church.

Vinco Mateljan, on the other hand, had no problem obtaining a visa for Australia in 1966 when his brother sponsored him and his wife Katerina and son Peter and paid their fares. At their home in Jandakot in 1997, Katerina related how she had to leave her daughter behind with her mother because it would have been difficult for her to work alongside her husband with a young child.

Many of the early Croatian immigrants had settled around the Manjimup district and taken up tobacco growing, supplementing their income with occasional work in the timber industry. However, a significant number moved further afield after the tobacco crops in Manjimup failed and the industry collapsed in 1961. As a result, Croatian arrivals towards the end of the decade tended to head to the eastern states where relatives and friends had established themselves. Zoran Panzich, a journalist in the Manjimup area in 1997, believed that the Croatian migration into Manjimup most probably ceased in the early sixties. Peter Radomiljac, whose father Marco had arrived in 1926, recalled his parents stating that there had been many Yugoslavs in the Manjimup district in the interwar period but there were very few Croatian families remaining in the area. Radomiljac believed that, as most of the early arrivals had worked as sleeper cutters in the bush, many such as Jack Surina had never married and they eventually died. Among the Yugoslav immigrants in the latter part of the decade were a significant number of Macedonians who entered the timber industry in the Manjimup district after arrival for a short period of time. During his interview in Manjimup in 1997, Norm Howe told me that Croatians:

> gradually worked their way out of it until they got something better. The mills were regarded as just a part-time sort of thing (a stepping stone), and when they could find something better to do, they left.

Italian migration: The ebb and flow

The rise in southern European migration to mid-1950s was so disturbing to Australian officials that in 1955 the small-scale assistance programmes for Italians were reduced. Sponsorship categories tightened so that Italians could sponsor only very close relatives instead of a wide range of friends and relations as had become the practice. Joe Crognale and Giacomo Fimmano both came to Western Australia in 1956. Fimmano was sponsored by one of his two brothers who lived in Harvey, and Crognale, despite the restrictions, was nominated by a friend from the same region in Italy.

Many newly-arrived Italians felt that Australian authorities had misled them with regard to employment opportunities. The Secretary of the newly-formed Italian Friendly Society in Western Australia, A. Strano, told local newspapers in 1956 that Italians were returning to Italy or migrating to the eastern states in ever increasing numbers because of rising unemployment. Italian immigration to Western Australia fell sharply in 1957 and then fluctuated with the occasional brief recovery to the late 1960s. Assisted passage and nomination schemes had favoured single male immigration. Many Italians sought to bring out their wives and families as soon as possible so that between 1957 and 1959 Italian female migration overtook male migration.

Table 8.2: Migration figures for Western Australia for Italians 1956-1968

Year	Arrivals			Departures			Excess of arrivals over departures
	Males	Females	Total	Males	Females	Total	
1956	2,299	863	3,162	300	13	313	2,849
1957	647	815	1,462	234	36	270	1,192
1958	409	857	1,266	296	52	348	918
1959	550	597	1,147	134	33	167	980
1960	1,149	678	1,827	147	30	177	1,650
1961	674	651	1,325	122	22	144	1,181
1962	803	719	1,522	144	46	190	1,332
1963	557	509	1,066	149	66	215	851
1964	420	456	876	189	74	263	613
1965	357	401	758	137	88	225	533
1966	471	378	849	141	80	221	628
1967	730	545	1,275	153	103	256	1,019
1968	759	546	1,305	195	133	328	977

Australian Bureau of Statistics

The Italian-Australian migration agreement

The Italian-Australian migration agreement was due for renewal in 1961, but the Italian government refused to sign until 1967 when Australia finally agreed to Italy's demands that Italians would be treated on the same basis as other immigrants. In the meantime, Italy did allow existing arrangements with regard to nominated dependents to continue to 1964. At the same time in 1962, the Immigration Department wrote to industry employers, organisations and statutory bodies such as the Forests Department to promote their "Sponsor a

Skilled Migrant" assisted passage scheme. This invitation was extended to all migrants from Britain or Europe to put forward the name of a relative or friend who appeared to be eligible for consideration under this scheme and wished to come to Australia. It was hoped that the sponsor would provide accommodation and assist in obtaining employment for the nominee.

In order to reduce the rate of emigration, the Federal government amended legislation to make settlement in Australia more attractive to groups such as Italians and Croatians. In 1962 it reduced the eligibility requirement for age pensions from twenty to ten years residency. Then in August 1966, discrimination in social security benefits based on citizenship status that applied to age, invalid and widows' pensions was finally removed. These efforts were not sufficient to stem the growing return migration.

Between 1960 and 1964 all the Italians that Benvenuto and Celso Gherardi had sponsored a decade earlier returned to Italy. According to Benvenuto,

> well, they went back because they thought maybe a better life over there.

Likewise, some of the Italians sponsored by Cesare Coli and Albert Piacentini returned to Italy after a few years in Australia. Until 1969, Italians did not enjoy the same rights as northern Europeans or Britons who were entitled to passage assistance to bring their families with them.

Assimilation

The growing numbers of Italians in Western Australia in the post-war period prompted criticism that these immigrants 'were not being effectively absorbed'. Speaking in defence of Italian immigrants, Dr S. Callea, Italian Vice-consul in Perth, stated that:

> It is hard for a man to take an active role in community activities when he is working long hours to get enough money for his family to join him.

In response to these concerns, the WA Italian Welfare Committee was established in January 1956 with representatives from the Australian and Italian governments and the community to assist the Italians to become integrated in the new life they had chosen in this country. The Department of Immigration was opposed to the formation of this committee, stating:

> Has the committee executive been advised of the "Services" available to assist in the promotion of migrant assimilation e.g. Adult migrant education scheme, the Good Neighbour Movement and the requirement of all non-Britishers to comply with the formalities relating to alien registration?

The Perth Immigration Department office warned that until such time as the committee became affiliated with the Good Neighbour Movement, its activities would 'be closely followed and subject of future reports'. This affiliation took place in December 1956, but the Department's actions had served to confirm views that the Department's main concern was compliance.

None of those interviewed who still resided in the south-west of the state had heard of organisations such as the Good Neighbour Council. This included Anglo-Australians such as Ron Kitson who, retired and living at his home in the south-west town of Pemberton in 1997, told me:

I've never heard of that Good Neighbour Movement down here. I've never ever heard of it!

Josip Grguric first came across the Good Neighbour Council when he moved to Fremantle from Nannup. He joined the organisation in the mid 1950s working with the Migrant Emergency Fund.

Integration

Amidst concerns that Australia was losing its attractiveness as an immigrant destination, a report entitled 'Cultural integration of migrants' found that ethnic clubs and organisations did not threaten the government's assimilation policies. By 1959, the rhetoric of conformity was toned down with the immigration department using the term integration rather than assimilation. This was accompanied by a shift in emphasis that migrants would not weaken the links with British tradition but enrich cultural life. It was not until 1964, however, that the term 'integration' was officially adopted.

Timber industry downturn

In the four year period to 1959, the Associated Sawmillers representing the large sawmilling companies reported 'extremely difficult trading conditions' at the overseas, interstate and local levels. With a drop in profit margins, sawmilling companies such as Bunning Bros embarked on a programme to modernise their plant and looked to diversification of their products to maintain profits and market presence.

This downturn was not uniform across the industry. In fact, the *West Australian* reported in August 1958 that small timber mills throughout the south-west were 'riding on the crest of an export trade boom' where only twelve months previously they had to put men off for lack of work. Italian and Croatian timber workers benefitted from this upturn. According to Tomasi, it was more a shortage of skilled labourers such as benchmen that affected the industry. Tomasi had taken up felling trees under contract in the Nannup area from 1959 with his two cousins:

> We were knocking down about a hundred loads a day each. .What we earn in one day, one week on wages we were earning in one day. We were making good money. We pay a lot of tax.

Their opportunities were short-lived, however. From 1959, many Italian and Croatian mill owners such as Italo Tomasi experienced greater difficulty in obtaining sufficient supplies from private properties. The situation was further aggravated through the importation by the eastern states of overseas timbers at cheaper prices resulting in less demand from these states for Western Australian timbers.

Forestry versus agriculture

The Brand Liberal government elected in 1959 combined the two portfolios of Lands and Forests under one Minister to obtain 'better balance than had hitherto existed' between the conflicting assertions of the Agricultural and Timber industries. Claims and counter claims over the most profitable use of forests land persisted over the period, with A.C. Harris, Conservator of Forests, stating in 1965:

> The inescapable fact, well known to foresters for many years, is that the farming community of the South West has an innate hostility to the forest, and to the controls necessary if forests are to be preserved. ...To farmers, the only development is agriculture. They refuse to regard the forest as a crop, or to acknowledge that you cannot continually whittle away the forest and preserve the timber industry.

The Minister for Forests reassured the timber industry representatives that the bringing together of the two portfolios was an effort to address the continual struggle between the forestry and agricultural industry over the utilisation of land in the best interests of the community. The Brand government also sought to encourage the growth of private forests and protect owners' timber rights. Tighter controls and specifications were introduced to distinguish between forestry and farming lands. These changes were intended to maintain a sustained yield which would:

> provide as far as possible, stability in the timber industry and guarantee continuity of employment and associated settlements and townships.

Stricter controls favoured the larger, established sawmills to the detriment of the smaller firms. As timber production fell, the number of registered sawmills followed suit. The *Harvey-Murray Times* captured the frustration of the small mill owners, dependent on contracts from the larger sawmilling firms who enjoyed a stranglehold over timber leases. Under the caption 'Closing down or curtailment of operations at over 50 mills in the south-west', the newspaper reported that a large number of men had been:

thrown out of employment and the outlook for the resumption of work at these mills (was) not bright.

When timber production again increased from 1964 there was no concurrent increase in the number of mills. According to Brian Easton, partner in the sawmilling firm Easton Barmell:

> the monopoly of trade in jarrah and karri was exercised by the selective issue of felling licences to Bunning and two small millers, which left Barmell with only Marri and small quantities of smaller species, for which there was little market demand.

Labour shortages in the timber industry

The labour situation which was so detrimental to the timber industry employers provided excellent opportunities for Italians and Croatian timber workers, especially as timber production increased from 1963. After re-emigrating to Australia in 1959, Jerko Grbavac was employed by Millars' mill in Quinninup and later transferred to its Jardee mill after a fire destroyed the Quinninup mill. Around 1964, with employment opportunities abounding, Grbavac moved from one mill site to the next. In his words,

> wherever they pay me better money, I go in there.

He worked at Joe Oregoni's mill in West Palgarup for about eighteen months before changing employment once again, first to work for Barmell Pty Ltd at its Jardee mill and later for John Mateljan in Dingup. Grbavac's frequent changes of employment were typical of the period reflected in the high turnover at mill sites.

Stipe Grubisin and his brother first went to work on their uncle's orchard in Bridgetown for a couple of weeks before moving to Peter Musulin's tobacco farm in Manjimup after they arrived in Fremantle in 1960. At the end of the tobacco season, they found work at a sawmill in Quinninup. After three months, Grubisin decided to move to another sawmill at Yornup and then changed workplace again after six months finding work at yet another small sawmill at Kulikup. Grubisin recalled that

> those days you had to move for the better pay. And that's what I did.

Within a few months he was back in Bridgetown this time working for Mate Pulis mainly as a faller. The small spot mills usually operated with a small workforce of four to six people, mostly Italians, with some Croatians and Macedonians and the occasional Australian. Most of the employees doubled up on various jobs and Grubisin sometimes operated the small bench, where he eventually lost a finger. He left Bridgetown and the timber industry in 1963 and moved to the banana industry in Carnarvon to join his brother and cousin.

Immigration drives by the large sawmilling companies

The nomination of relatives by those already working at mills was a source of labour that had been used with a good degree of success in the early 1950s. However, many Italians had moved on to 'better prospects' and, with resistance from Italian authorities, this source did not yield sufficient numbers. Thus by the mid-1960s, the Associated Sawmillers and Timber Merchants (Associated Sawmillers) turned once again to displaced people of Yugoslav origin to secure workers. They wrote to the Department of Labour requesting an immigrant intake of ten per month to cover labour turnover in the timber industry. Immigrants would be recruited from ships arriving at Fremantle to Millars' mill in Quinninup where they would be housed and assessed as to their suitability for various jobs and receive some basic training over a two to three week period before proceeding to employment with a particular mill.

Alarmed with growing return migration, the Department of Labour advised:

> I trust that the employers concerned fully understand that the Commonwealth cannot direct migrants to employment and can only use persuasive powers to induce them to take employment in country centres and remote areas. It is not realistic nowadays to speak about allocations of labour being made from migrant intakes or to encourage employers to believe that this can be done.

Ben Bryant, retired and living in the Perth suburb of Nedlands in 1997, recalled the changing ethnic composition of the timber industry workforce during this period. He reflected that the:

> Italian content dried up a little for a while and more Yugoslavs came out.

Bryant remembered visiting the ships that called into Fremantle to persuade some of the Yugoslav refugees to disembark and go to work at the mill. Those so persuaded would be housed at Graylands for a few days whilst Bryant organised transport to Nyamup:

> There'd be a man and his wife and a child or two, and

all they had in the world was in a suitcase. ..I would provide them with the basic living requirements. Beds and a kitchen table and chairs, pots and pans and things like that to start off.

Timber industry labour turnover

Notwithstanding all the efforts made to recruit workers and to establish a more stable workforce, the turnover of labour in the large sawmilling companies remained a major cause for concern. In the year to November 1965 the industry recorded a turnover rate of 86.2%. One of the issues identified was supervisory attitudes especially towards the growing Italian and Croatian workforce. Stipe Grubisin recalled that in most of the large sawmills all the foremen and 'leading hands' were Australian:

> Maybe because we couldn't speak English. Well they sort of keep you as second class citizen or people. The only thing I used to understand is dago bastard. Some of them wasn't so friendly with persons who couldn't speak.

According to Zoran Panzich:

> The Australian content was almost negligible, except for management, for booking keeping and ...for those roles. The actual physical work situation I'd say was 90% foreigners, almost an even mix of Slavs and Italians over the period'.

With increasing concentration of production from the large established sawmills, opportunities for the small mills decreased. As a result, many Italians and Croatians moved into the larger mills in ever increasing numbers as Anglo-Australians found work in other less remote locations of Western Australia. This shift meant that there was less opportunity for Italians and Croatians to move into mill ownership, but it also influenced the handling of Italian and Croatian mill workers. Recognising that a more stable workforce would yield benefits in productivity and levels of earnings, the Associated Sawmillers introduced changes to their workforce management. It brought about the start of significant cultural change in the treatment of immigrant workers by employers, supervisors and fellow workers.

9

Growing Roots

Despite adverse conditions, the Western Australian timber industry still ranked third to wool and wheat in value of primary products in 1965, and the state supplied 75% of timber exports from the Commonwealth. With the supply of hardwoods diminishing, the Forests Department stepped up its pine plantation programme so that, by 1969, pine production accounted for roughly 9% of total timber production for that year. Sawmilling companies introduced greater mechanisation and automation as they turned to manufactured wood products such as particle board, plywood and veneer to maintain profitability. Notwithstanding the high degree of mechanisation of sawmills and the fact wages rose about 26% from 1960 to 1968, labour was still hard to attract.

Forest industries work

Whilst sawmilling was the main forest industry, the so-called minor forest industries produced roughly one quarter of the value of sawn timber production. These included mining timber, charcoal supply, wandoo for the production of tannin extract and sandalwood. Italo Tomasi held a timber salvage licence which entitled him to collect all the timber up to his licence limit in salvage situations such as wherever land had been cleared by a bulldozer as in the case when roads were put through the forests, and when wind damage had knocked trees over. Italo and his two cousins, Fred and John Tomasi, purchased their own spot mill from a Croatian called John Mateljan in 1967. They employed five men, two Yugoslavs, Vinco Mateljan and Jimmy Lazarevic, two Italians - one of whom was the benchman Jim Del Borello, and 'an English'. Vinco Mateljan had been sponsored by his brother Peter in 1966. He worked at the Kundenup mill for seven years, first for his cousin John Mateljan and later for Italo Tomasi.

Firewood production averaged 705,000 tons to the end of the 1960s of which approximately 56 per cent was for domestic consumption. Benvenuto Gherardi and his brother Celso operated a firewood and carting company to around 1969. Most of the time they carted jarrah from Jarrahdale and banksia from Peel Estate and Karnup but they also worked for the transport company Bell Brothers in between transporting wood. At his home in the Perth suburb of Beaconsfield in 1996, Benvenuto recalled how he had been ticked off by the forestry inspector for not properly and promptly recording the tonnage in the log book provided by the Forests Department for which royalty was payable:

> Sometimes when we come out of the bush, we supposed to put down, hours, so and so.. (in the) log book. Sometimes we forget. ..I used to take the clothes with me to get changed when I get wet, so I not stay wet all day, see. .put dry clothes and then come home.. One day I was in Jarrahdale, he (the inspector) was

there, stopped me and said, you show the book. Ah, forgot to put down.. but then he tell me, "you forget to have breakfast this morning?"

Over one million linear feet of piles and poles used for purposes such as the construction of jetties, harbour works, rail and road bridges, and telegraph lines were obtained annually from Crown land and private property. Aged 65 in 1997, Crognale, who started out chopping trees for telegraph and electricity poles, still worked for the same employer, Vincenzo Ridolpho. Over the years he had worked in whatever capacity was needed, as bull dozer driver, truck driver, faller, tree marker and pole cutter among others.

Towards the end of the decade, particularly in the smaller spot mills, the workers were almost exclusively continental Europeans with a high percentage of Italians, Croatians and Macedonians at many mill sites. At the Jardee mill owned by Barmell Pty Ltd, for example, the workforce in 1968-69 was '99% Macedonian' which Norm Howe, an Australian bulldozer driver who was employed by Barmell's mill, stated was 'normal' at the time.

The last bastion

One of the last bastions of resistance to continental European labour was the Forests Department's workforce. In fact, when it implemented a recruitment drive to overcome labour shortages in 1967 it looked no further than the United Kingdom. Under an assisted passage scheme, 65 British immigrants (including wives and children) were brought out. At the end of the decade, Italians and Croatians made up only 7% of the total Forests Department workforce of 402 employees, among whom were Peter Radomiljac, Cosimo Ventrici and Giacomo Fimmano. Radomiljac was born in Australia at the outbreak of the Second World War. His father, Marco, had been one of the early interwar arrivals into the timber industry and his mother was Australian. At the Manjimup office of the Department of Conservation and Land Management, where Peter was still employed in 1997, he told of his great love for the Australian bush:

> There was plenty of work around, .them days, but I liked to work where the real physical work was. I was born to work in the bush and that's the sort of work I looked for.

Radomiljac's first work was clearing land around Manjimup and helping out on his father's tobacco farm before moving into the timber industry full-time at Deanmill in 1958. He worked there until 1964 when he decided to join the Forests Department in Manjimup, building roads and bridges, doing regeneration work and burning, planting trees in the wintertime and any other work that was required to maintain the forests.

Ventrici and Fimmano, both post-war arrivals, joined the Forests Department in the 1960s working in the bush in the Harvey district. In the early 1960s, the Department had a pine sawmill and Fimmano worked inside the mill for a number of years until he was ordered by his doctor to work outside the mill due to ear trouble. Fimmano recalled that there were several Italian, Polish and Yugoslav workers employed as casuals for short periods, and sometimes these groups made up roughly 30 per cent of the workforce in the bush. The office workers were '*tutti Australiani*' [all Australians].

Women into the timber industry workforce

Another strategy to overcome labour shortages was the recruitment of women into the timber industry workforce. From around 1964, sawmill managers employed:

> females ...taking over lighter jobs and working on some of the less complicated machines.

Women were introduced into the timber workshops of the large mills which produced prefabricated materials, timber joinery and other timber produce. It was anticipated that they would eventually proceed to key mill jobs such as bench operators. According to Italo Tomasi, Jerko and Blgica Grbavac and others, women were not to be found in the small mills. At Barmell's Jardee mill, however, one third of the workforce were women. In the Harvey district, Giacomo Fimmano recalled that several 'English' women were employed at local sawmills:

> non fare pesante lavoro. Giusto a staccare timber, due per tre, uno per due. [Not doing heavy work. Only stacking timber, two by three, one by two].

Italian and Croatian women often worked very hard especially at weekends helping their husbands in whatever work was available, including in timber industry work. Her diminutive size did not stop Vincenzina Crognale working alongside her husband with an axe between 1962 and 1968. During the week, her husband Giacinto cut the trees down, measured them up and cut them into posts or poles and, on weekends, Vincenzina would 'take off the skin ..very hard work'. This entailed removing the bark by axe. Vincenzina would then bind the tops and bottoms of the posts so the timber would not split and grease them. She was often assisted by her young son who was eight years of age when he joined them 'de-barking' trees after school.

Katerina Mateljan worked in Italo Tomasi's Kundenup mill for three years, 'greasing sleepers' to prevent the timber from cracking. She was paid piece rates and although it was 'not much, it still help us'. In 1970 she went to work at Millars' mill in Nannup. Katerina worked in the pre-fabricated building section which produced window and door frames, flooring and other timber building products. She started work at seven o'clock in the morning and recalled that:

> it was very hard, you know. Kids have to make it selves to the school. I never see the kids in the morning going to school, and kids coming before me from school.

Blgica Grbavac also worked alongside her husband on tobacco farms whenever she had the time during the week and on most weekends to complement his wages from the timber yard in Quinninup. The interviewees often stressed the hardships they endured to achieve financial security and home ownership.

Supplementing their income

One of the enduring themes in the interviews was the extra work that the Italian and Croatian men and women undertook in order to establish themselves in Australia. Vinco Mateljan, for example, started his day at:

> four o'clock in the morning and finish eight o'clock night time. About fourteen, fifteen hours a day, every day, never stop, never stop.

Mateljan was paid by contract according to the loads of timber he produced. It was not unusual for him to earn $160 in a week, towards the end of the decade, when the basic wage for male labourers in the timber industry was $36. Jerko Grbavac summed up the stories of many, recalling that:

> From the day I start working at the mill, I never stopped working. No Saturday, no Sunday, every day working overtime on the mill. If I haven't got job on the mill, I work on a farm, cleaning farm, cleaning sticks, rocks, ...drive the trucks .or even make a silage for people. For every farmer ...was weekend, ...split the wood for curing tobacco.

According to his wife Blgica:

> the fathers there (in the mills) and they bought the farm and still paying slowly with the tobacco. Then their sons grow up or bring it from the old country. Then their sons went on the mill and making money extra, on top, and wives, and all of them working paying off the farms.

The multiplicity of workplaces was also necessitated by other factors. Peter Radomiljac made the point that:

> In those days you had to do it because if one thing failed, you had a bit of back-up with another one that came along. You had to mix farm in them days because they were only small farmers. You couldn't just rely on the tobacco industry to bring in your income for twelve months, or your dairy, or your potato crop ...and we had to look for new markets, new buyers, outside Australia, and that doesn't happen overnight.

Radomiljac believed that the 'starting point' for most

new arrivals was the mills which, although declining in numbers especially during the 1960s, were numerous enough for Radomiljac to recall 'each corner was a mill working'. Italians and Croatians:

> got into those little mills, they worked five or ten years, ..learnt to speak English, learnt to know the place, learnt to make friends ..new ideas and where the better prospects were and that's what they headed for.

Domenic Anzellino, who had migrated to Australia in 1951 at eight years of age and attended school at Yarloop, started work at Millars' yard as a sixteen-year-old office boy. Anzellino 'wanted to make lots of money' and so asked the foreman for work in the yard stacking timber. He spent approximately fourteen years in the timber yard before moving to carpentry and eventually becoming a foreman after 1970.

Few Italians and Croatians reached the rank of foreman. One exception was Peter Ucich, who was foreman at Millars' Hoffman Mill (later moved to Yarloop) from 1958 until his retirement in 1985. Giacomo Fimmano still worked for the Forests Department (Department of Conservation and Land Management) in 1997 and, reflecting the views of many, felt that Australians were given preference in employment opportunities. In Joe Celisano's view:

> I don't think that was fair because we all pay the same tax. We emigrate here through the right channels and everything and I don't think that was right. That didn't happen too often, but it did happen.

Work exploitation

Post-war Italian and Croatian workers in the timber

industry generally did not encounter issues such as non-payment for work and the poor working conditions that were so prevalent in the interwar years. One exception was Giacinto Crognale who cut trees for posts and poles on private property in 1960. As timber from this source grew scarce, Crognale recalled that times were:

> very, very bad.. the money does come, he (Crognale's employer) not make enough what he spent for food. Well you have to eat something. I have no boots. I work through the bush for weeks and weeks, no boots on my foot. The boots, the mud ..he did for me. Three days, no main meals, ..just water. If you don't believe that, I swear now, because now a big company, but he no look after what I did.

Crognale went for six months without pay after which time he told his boss, Vincenzo Ridolpho, that he was quitting his job. When Crognale returned to the south-west after a few months in the northern part of the state, Ridolpho approached him once again to work for him, assuring Crognale that he was no longer in the partnership which had cost both of them so much, Crognale having lost his 'ute' and his house in the process. Crognale still worked for Ridolpho when interviewed in 1997.

Dangerous work

Well into the 1960s, timber work was still 'very dangerous work' with little training for the Italian and Croatian recruits into this industry. Safety issues were never considered when they were 'out in the bush', handling logs and timber, hauling or loading/unloading the trucks, or working the larger benches in the timber mills. Peter Radomiljac pointed out that:

> We didn't have safety boots, them days. There was no such things as helmets, ear muffs. There was nothing. It was just the clothes on your back and away you went.

Leone Spiccia and Antony La Manna were travelling on a 'box type seat' on the back of a truck on their way home from work at Mundaring on 22 October 1963. The two men were 'thrown heavily onto the bitumen road' as the truck rounded a sharp bend and the seat, which was nailed to the floor, came loose. As a result, Spiccia sustained head injuries from which he died four days later and La Manna received a fractured skull and pelvis and was unconscious for two days. The Spiccia/La Manna accident was preventable and highlighted the lack of safety rules which prompted the industry to review all work processes and safety standards. The timber industry generally, however, was slow to respond to safety measures. A recommendation in 1965 by the National Safety Council for the Sawmillers' Association to appoint a full time safety officer was not taken up. It was felt that the control of safety matters should 'more rightfully rest with individual companies'.

Donnelly River Mill was the first Bunning Bros mill site to establish a Safety Committee in the early 1960s. The members were drawn from across all divisions or sections in the mill, yards, bush and workshops and were not restricted to foremen. As a result of the committee's work, a safety education induction programme for new and inexperienced employees was drawn up.

Following from the successful outcomes at Donnelly River which achieved an average 28% reduction in accident rates, Bunning Bros appointed a full time safety officer in Manjimup in March 1966. Through the implementation of a comprehensive accident prevention programme, the company was able to dramatically reduce the number of accidents in its six sawmills spread over the south west of the state. Bunnings (Nyamup) became the first sawmill in the state to achieve 250,000 man hours worked (460 working days) without a 'Lost Time Injury' in August 1969.

The accident rate in those sectors of the industry where accident prevention programmes were introduced decreased by 50% over two years. Unfortunately in some of the smaller mills, safety measures remained a low priority. Barmell's mill in Jardee was, for instance:

> typical of the older timber mills in the South-West. Most machinery was twenty five years old or more and safety standards were minimal. There was little in the way of mechanical handling in the mill after the first log trim operation.

The Forests Department appointed a full-time safety officer in 1966 and achieved the same spectacular results. Within three years, the annual frequency rate of accidents fell from 102 to 37 and the number of days lost fell from 2,896 to 721. In addition, from 1969 the department was more vigilant in ensuring the registration of all sawmills and in maintaining inspection of sawmills.

The Italians and Croatians entering the industry were aware of the dangerous nature of the work. In Stipe Grubisin's words:

> Of course that was dangerous, but in those days you didn't think of it, what's dangerous. You had to earn, because when you're a stranger in a strange country, strange language, you have to do something to stay on your two feet.

Those who sustained injuries also complained about the inadequate compensation schemes. Jerko Grbavac had just moved into his new home in Manjimup when he lost an arm whilst working at John Mateljan's mill in Dingup in 1969. With four young children to raise, his wife was devastated. She told me:

> I worked. I cleaning houses, scrubbing .and polishing and ironing .for five dollars for five hours on my knees ..and look everywhere I can get a job, an hour or two picking apples or *patates*. I come home, I couldn't stand on my feet. Next morning my back sore but I still stand up next to the wall to straighten myself out and pretending nothing wrong with me.

Her husband explained that:

> When they pay the $7,000 money, compensation ..which went into the bank because we have the house, and every penny I have at that time I pay the house everything. Nothing left. Bank manager ask me what about living, I say no. If you take my hand, house is mine. But if I got money your dollar in my pocket, you got title on house, house is not mine.

Jerko and Blgica Grbavac received a government pension after nine months. However, Jerko also discovered that he had lost his hearing due to the high pitched noise of the twin saws at the mill. The nature of the hearing loss was such that hearing aids could not be used and he had to put up with a high pitched whining noise thereafter. This type of affliction was very common among mill workers. When interviewed in 1997, Ben Bryant was also affected by hearing loss and suffered the same discomfort.

Housing and amenities

Housing and amenities for timber industry workers continued to improve for most timber workers. In spite of this, many new arrivals found living conditions difficult to accept. Katerina Mateljan, for example, remembered the first house close to the Kundenup mill where her husband worked:

> It was very awful. Winter time.. not a shower, not a toilet, it's everything outside. We have to boil all the water in a copper, and we have concrete bath, and we bring it with buckets and put it in the bath. Before I put Peter (her son) in for the wash, that water, it's cold.

Her husband recalled having to continuously move the bed around when it rained in order to avoid all the leaks in the roof. The result was that the house was not only 'very cold' but also damp. Katerina Mateljan felt 'very bad, never sleep' after arrival but reflected:

> still, me coming here for work, for make money, for better, family. Here good future.

Isolated settlements were gradually moved to larger centres of population and workers commuted by bus or other forms of transport. As part of his childhood years in the town of Manjimup, Zoran Panzich remembered one Macedonian in particular who used to cycle one and a half kilometres into town every morning to where the bus from Nyamup mill would pick them up. The bus collected some twenty men, none of whom were 'English people'.

With the recruiting of increasing numbers of immigrants from ships, basic household necessities such as cooking utensils, bedding and furniture were included upon arrival at the mill site. This equipment was purchased by the sawmilling company and the workers would repay the costs from wages over a period of time. At the Nyamup mill, it was estimated that the company outlay averaged £10 for a single man and ranged to £150 for a married couple with children. The benefit of this outlay was that the immigrants would remain in the employ of the Company on a reasonably permanent basis and bring stability to the workforce. From 1968, the Forests Department and some of the larger sawmilling companies turned to transportable timber framed cottages to meet the demand for housing in the south-west timber areas.

Women and children

It was often much harder for the women and the children, especially those who lived in milling towns. Blgica Grbavac, who came to Quinninup mill immediately after arrival from Croatia in 1960, recalled that she really regretted coming to Australia:

> The neighbours in Quinninup, they are joking when my kids talk my language, and they tell us all kind, you know, pretend we are like animals not like people. And they take my kids and start to fight them and put dirt on them.
> When you come on verandah, you scared to look at them (the Australian men) because they call you names. But when you don't understand what they said, what you bitch staring on?
> I didn't think so I make it here. Five years.. I be very happy if I make it five years.

Norm Howe, an employee at the Quinninup mill,

supported Blgica's views stating that some of the Australians on the mill site were:

> a bit rough in their language towards the women and sometimes a bit abusive.

Croatian and Italian children were also targeted in the school grounds and on the sports fields and both Peter Radomiljac and Zoran Panzich recalled:

> we were called dings, wogs, dagos, you name it, we were called it.

Earlier in the interview, Radomiljac stated that 'there was no spice', and all races 'blended together' well. Towards the end of the interview he acknowledged that 'ah yes, there was racism for sure' pointing out this occurred particularly on the sports fields . Panzich felt that he was somewhat protected from the worst racist elements at the Catholic school he attended in Manjimup but:

> going into the high school system was a nightmare. It was so difficult that I can't even begin to describe it.

Language

Language was always a major stumbling block and usually, the older the immigrant the greater the problem to learn English. Zoran Panzich recalled accompanying his father to English classes in Jardee. His father:

> never really got the swing of English. He was most probably too old to learn it. ..they were reliant upon their own physical being.

In Panzich's view, his dad would have taken up work other than in the timber industry, but 'he didn't have that choice'.

Several men found themselves isolated in small timber communities surrounded by few Australians. Vinco Mateljan, for example, spent the first seven years working in Kundenup with 'no English people. Only Italian, Croatian and Slovenian', and he 'no hear English for seven years'. Although his Italian did improve during this period, Mateljan reflected that English was always 'very problem'. Very few persevered with lessons and most of the men learnt English 'just practising with the people'.

Lack of English often meant that Italians and Croatians were never able to express their point of view and had to accept orders unquestioningly. Giacinto Crognale summed up the frustration of most:

> you can't understand, you ask something, you can't answer back.. see you can't tell the boss whatever, you have to do it. You reckon you do it right, ..was wrong. He told you what you have to do, you can't understand. ..you work hard, ..try more hard, always you wrong, because that's very hard, the first we start.

Fimmano spoke of the lack of choice for Italians and Croatians:

> *Non c'era choice perche a quei tempi dove diceva il boss ..se deve fare questo, e nessuno parlava. Se faceva e si finiva. Oggi, magari, si po dire a una persona non posso fare questo. Te davano un altro. Ma a quei tempi non aveva scelta.* [There was no choice because in those days where the boss said you had to do that, and nobody spoke. You did it and finished it. Today, perhaps, you can tell a person I cannot do that. They

give you something else. But during those times there was no choice].

Intercultural relations

Milling centres such as Manjimup were often quite biased against Italians and Croatians. At his farm outside Manjimup in 1997 where Jerko Panzich, at the age of 75, still helped his son, Panzich stated that some Australians

> couldn't see the foreigners, calling them names and fight with them, you name it, right in the town.

Panzich recalled that businessmen

> did start to come round, because they could see the foreigners were bringing the money in.

Jerko was part of a band of young Yugoslav boys who were often asked to play at dances:

> Saturdays, I used to go to the dances, and these young Australians would stand at the door to belt them up as they walked out. ..We were on stage, and three of them stood at the door and Vic, my brother, says to me, watch out, we got a problem. So instead of folding the music stand, we take each one in the hand ...they could see we not packing them like usual and as we approached the door, they just moved aside.

Name calling was still quite prevalent but most Italians and Croatians believed the best response was 'to just keep quiet'. What annoyed Italo Tomasi most was Australians picking on Italians using their hands when speaking, which prompted his retort:

> I'd like the Australian go in Italy, how they prepare

themselves. They have to work with their hands too. They got to explain themselves.

Others such as Giacinto Crognale found the name calling 'stupid'. He confronted one shop owner:

> you call me "ding" all the time. Where I am now? I am Australian like you. What you call me now?'

Crognale told me that, try as he could, he knew that he would always be seen as 'foreign' by some. Ron Kitson, an Anglo-Australian who had been a bush worker during the 1950s, regarded name calling quite differently. He dismissed it as mutual poking of fun, stating that 'we were all good mates, you know'.

There is evidence of growing cross cultural awareness in the timber industry towards the end of the decade. At Barmell's Jardee mill, on the occasion of a feast day in the Greek Orthodox church, the mill site came to a standstill for the day. Brian Easton recalled the day's events:

> a bishop of that Church arrived at the mill and was ceremoniously conducted round the establishment, blessing each work station and its occupant as he proceeded. After each blessing the operative fell in at the tail of the procession which terminated at Jardee station where a spread was prepared and some traditional dancing occurred, the dancers in traditional costume.

Despite these developments, many of those interviewed expressed the view that, at the time of the interviews in 1997, there was still a strong undercurrent of resentment directed towards them by Australians. Perhaps the most salient point was made by Stefania Rijavec:

> *Siamo qui, noi vecchi, sempre come foreigner, never come viene, venire dentro, sempre come foreigner..* [We're here, we elderly people, always as foreigner, never how it should be, come inside, always as foreigner].

With economic independence as their goal, Italians and Croatians endured long working hours and tolerated harsh living conditions. Yet, achieving their goals had its downside. In Joe Celisano's words:

> in the end of the day we had a lot of questions from Australian people say, you come here, you can't speak, you had nothing, we were working together, how come you buy house, I didn't?
> I think they see me always as Italian. But that's natural I suppose. They see Japanese always as Japanese, and they see Asians as Asians.

If some Australians were envious of gains made by Italians and Croatians, then there was a sense of vindication among the latter groups when they and their children achieved upward mobility and/or financial security. Blgica and her husband Jerko Grbavac, for example, were upset when their children were teased, picked and set upon and jeered for 'talking funny':

> My kids talk now funny, but after they will be better than you. And time is come, my son teach that grandchildren of that person what they tell us.

These views took the form of pride in showing their children's achievements and accomplishments, a factor in almost every interview where the person had children. In Zoran Panzich's case, his father made the point bluntly when he told his son:

> You either go to school and learn and become educated or you do what I do. It's your choice.

Australian citizenship and dual identity

All my informants took up Australian citizenship. Many, such as Joe Celisano, Guy Ciappalone and Domenic Anzellino hoped that as naturalised subjects they would not be discriminated against and be entitled to all benefits. Celisano expressed the view that as he had made up his mind to stay in Australia, he 'might as well be naturalised and become a real Aussie'. He also cited another reason:

> I was on the job and they was putting people off work. Oh, if so and so not naturalised, he should not be working here. They would say, oh, he's not naturalised, he got a job. I'm Australian, they give me the boot.

Italo Tomasi told me that:

> Today, when I'm with the Australian, talk Australian. When I'm down at the Italian club, I talk Italian. No make no difference. Talking with the wife, we talk English. When we don't want the kids to understand, which they understand, we talk Italian, sometimes. They understand this too.

This view was shared by Benvenuto and his wife Edda Gherardi who felt 'more or less' Australian.

> Now I been out here 60 years, so more or less I feel (for) the country here more than the country over there. ..Well, you done all the work here. You live here. Family here. I wouldn't go back over there to live

because the style of living, could be better, but it wouldn't be the same for me. Been used to live over here.

His wife Edda, however, added that they still 'don't let go' their culture and often met up with Italian friends with whom they shared wine making, sausage making and other typical Italian cultural customs. For Jerko Panzich, it was a question of respect for other nationalities: 'I respect Yugoslavs, that's my nationality, but I belong to here'. As far as Stipe Grubisin was concerned, however:

> I feel I am Croatian, because I was born there. You never forget that. It doesn't matter how good living is here, you still got some sort of feeling for those days and for that country. I am citizen of Australia but I'm still Croatian. I can't say any different. I respect Australia very much because Australia especially today is country which respect everyone, doesn't matter what nationality or what religion you are. But those days was different.

This view was echoed by Giacomo Fimmamo:

> *Io sono nell'Australia e non posso parlare male dell'Australia. Ma non posso parlare nemmeno male della mia patria. I don't care se sono di cento anni o di cinquanta anni, la patria, non posso mai dimenticare* [I am in Australia and cannot speak badly of Australia. But I also cannot speak ill of my native country. I don't care if it was one hundred years or fifty years, my native land, I can never forget].

One benefit Fimmano enjoyed from taking up Australian citizenship was the ability to obtain a gun licence to go hunting rabbits.

'New Australian'

Those of the interviewees who used the term 'New Australian' to describe their status as new arrivals spoke of their contribution to this country. Katerina and Vinco Mateljan interpreted the term literally stating that they felt:

> New Australian all right.. feel very awful because no got nothing, like falling from a parachute, come in the middle of the bush and nothing and start new life, and working, working, together me and my wife.

They identified economic independence and stability as the characteristics making Australia 'best country in the world'. Zoran Panzich saw the term differently:

> I didn't really know what they meant except the word 'new' and 'Australian' means someone who just got here. But they were not terms of endearment. They still aren't. They were terms of put-down. They were more racist and more anti-migrant than they were conciliatory in the way that they were put towards you.

At the Grbavac's home in Manjimup in 1997, Norm Howe reflected that 'I call them all New Australians'. Notwithstanding the advances in accommodation of Italians and Croatians, their ethnicity was still the key identifier to their identity, and their status, in Australian society.

There is no disputing that the first half of the previous century, particularly during the depression period, saw some very tough times for the fledgling state of Western Australia. Italians and Croatians encountered prejudice, antagonism and exploitation. Whether as aliens, naturalised British subjects, naturalised aliens, and New Australians they were welcomed grudgingly into the periphery of the labour market in times of need, where they would not displace Australians. From the late 1950s, many reflected their disillusionment by returning to their countries of origin, a response that prompted the Australian government to reassess its treatment and obligations towards these groups. Even more turned to naturalisation as one way of bridging the cultural gap.

In so many of their interviews, Italians and Croatians detailed the difficult times and the hard work as challenges they had to endure to lay the foundation for a secure future for themselves and their families. Many felt that they attained their goal of economic independence and provided a basis for the achievements of their children - a great source of pride that resonated through so many of their stories.

The contribution of Italian and Croatian men and women to the development of the south-west of Western Australia in particular was significant. In search of a better life for them and their families, they took on whatever work was available, regardless of how remote, hard or dangerous. They opened up land for settlement and contributed to building its communities, growing roots throughout the State's south-west and beyond and earning their place among the early settlers who helped build Western Australia.

Italo Tomasi with logs, Kundenup 1969 *(photo courtesy I. Tomasi)*

Vinco Mateljan at Tomasi's sawmill, Kundenup 1969 *(photo courtesy V. Mateljan)*

Da Re's sawmill, Greenbushes 1969 *(photo courtesy V. Da Re)*

Frank Da Re (left) and Vittorio Da Re, Greenbushes 1969 *(photo courtesy V. Da Re)*

Oral Interviews

Mate Alac, Tuart Hill, 9 September 1995.
Domenico (Dom) Anzellino, Yarloop, 28 February 1997.
Cosimo (Charlie) Audino, Yarloop, 28 February 1997.
Tahir (Tom) Bajrovic, Hilton, 25 March 1997.
Pietro Baruffi (and daughter Nellie Giacci), Gelorup, 26 July 1995.
Bruce Beggs, Booragoon (Conservator of Forests, 1972-83), 18 March 1996.
Luigi Bertelli, Bunbury, 25 July 1995.
Maria Bordin, Leederville, 3 September 1996.
Ben Bryant, Nedlands, 17 February 1997.
Saverio Bruzzese, Belmont, 25 September 1996.
Josie Carzoli, Manjimup, 28 July 1995.
Joe Celisano, Harvey, 28 February 1997.
Guy Ciappalone, Bunbury, 27 February 1997.
Cesare and Esther Coli, Osborne Park, 11 September 1995.
Giacinto (Joe) and Vincenzina Crognale, Harvey, 28 February 1997.
Vittorio and Lidia Da Re, Bunbury, 26 February 1997.
Giuseppe D'Attilo, Maylands (Interview conducted by M. Bosworth), June 1990.
Basileo Dell'Agostino, Bunbury, 25 July 1995.
Brian Easton, Claremont, Note dated 21 October 1996.
Giacomo (Jack) Fimmano, Harvey, 28 February 1997.

Benvenuto Gherardi, Beaconsfield, 9 September 1996.
Jerko (Gerry) and Blgica Grbavac, Manjimup, 4 March 1997.
Josip Grguric, Kardinya, 22 March 1997.
Stipe Grubisin, Spearwood, 24 March 1997.
Ernest Hedington, Forestfield, 19 September 1996.
Norm Howe, Manjimup, 4 March 1997.
Keith Kessell, Perth, 15 February 1996.
Ron Kitson, Pemberton, 4 March 1997.
Joan Ladhams, Manjimup, 28 July 1995.
Angelo Marchesi, Perth, 6 September 1996.
Sam Marocchi, Perth 30 August 1996.
Vinco (and son Peter) Mateljan, Jandakot, 28 March 1997.
Vince Nani, Bunbury, 28 July 1995.
Giuseppe (Joe) and Mary Palandri, Margaret River, 29 July 1995.
Antonio Paparone, Fremantle, 9 September 1996.
Jerko (Gerry) and Catherina (Cath) Panzich, Manjimup, 5 March 1997.
Zoran Panzich, Manjimup, 4 March 1997.
Vincenzo Paternostro, Morley, 5 September 1996.
Vito Pesce, Bunbury, 1 March 1997.
Eva Polich, Manjimup, 5 March 1997.
Albert Piacentini, Glen Iris, 29 July 1995.
Else Charlotte Radomiljac, Manjimup, 27 July 1995.
Peter Radomiljac, Manjimup, 6 March 1997.
Stefania Rijavec, Manjimup, 27 July 1995.
Mara Sambrailo, Attadale, 8 November 1995 and 14 November 1995.
John Scott, Dalkeith, 30 January 1997.
Alfredo Strano, Balcatta, July 1997 and April 1998.
Jack Surina, Donnelly River, 28 July 1995.
Zuva Telenta (Interview conducted by M. Sambrailo).

Italo Tomasi, Bunbury, 26 February 1997.
Peter Ucich, Harvey, 30 July 1995.
Steve (and Mary) Viskovich, Millenden, 4 August 1995.
Rosa and Cosimo Ventrici, Harvey, 28 February 1997.
Rose Vlahov (Interview conducted by M. Sambrailo), 4 July 1990.

Bibliography

Manuscript Sources

Western Australian Government department files covering Forestry and Land Settlement in Western Australia 1917-1970

Commonwealth Files relating to Immigration, Internment, Prisoners of War over the period 1917-1970.

Australian Council of Trade Unions (ACTU): Decisions of the Australian Congress of Trade Unions, Melbourne, 1952 and 1967.

Bunning Bros Pty Ltd Annual Reports 1952-1970.

Newspapers/Magazines

Albany Advertiser.
Blackwood Times.
Coastal Times.
Countryman.
Daily News (formerly Weekend News).
Harvey-Murray Times.
South Western Times.
South West News.
Sunday Independent.
Timberlines.

Walkabout.
Western Mail.
West Australian.
West Australian News.

Secondary Sources

Alac, M., original manuscript, 'I love life so much: that's why I refuse to die' (1989) later *Into the World*, Fremantle Arts Centre Press, 1992.

Appleyard, R. T., 'Displaced Persons in Western Australia', *University Studies in History and Economics*, 2 (3) September, 1955.

Borrie, W.D., *Immigration: Australia's Problems and Prospects*, Sydney: Angus & Robertson, 1949.

- *Italians and Germans in Australia: A Study of Assimilation*, Melbourne: Cheshire (ANU), 1954.

Bosworth, R. & Ugolini, R. (eds), *War, Internment and Mass Migration: The Italo-Australian Experience 1940-1990*, Rome: Gruppo Editoriale Internazionale, 1992.

Bosworth, R., 'Cop what lot? A study of Australian attitudes towards Italian mass migration in the 1950s' in *Studi Emigrazioni*, xx (1983), pp. 37-57.

- 'Conspiracy of the Consuls? Official Italy and the Bonegilla Riot of 1952' in *Historical Studies*, Vol. 22, No. 89, October 1987.

Bunbury, B., *Rabbits and Spaghetti, Captives and Comrades: Australians, Italians and the War, 1939-1945*, Fremantle Arts Centre Press, 1995.

Castles, S., Alcorso, C., Rando, G., & Vasta, E. (eds), *Australia's Italians: Culture and Community in a Changing Society*, Sydney: Allen & Unwin, 1992.

Ciccotosto, E. & Bosworth, M., *Emma: A Translated Life*, Fremantle: Fremantle Arts Centre Press, 1990.

Cresciani, G., 'Australia, Italy and Italians, 1845-1945', *Studi Emigrazione*, XX, Rome: March 1983, No. 69.

Creswell, G. J., *The Light of Leeuwin*, Perth: Scott Four Colour Print for Augusta-Margaret River Shire History Group, 1989.

Curthoys, A. & Markus, A. (eds), *Who Are Our Enemies? Racism and the Australian Working class*, Sydney: Hale & Iremonger, 1978.

Czeladka, E.I., 'Yugoslavs in the Swan Valley and their Involvement in Viticulture', in *Aspects of Ethnicity in Western Australia*, Studies in Western Australian History, Vol. XII, April 1991.

de Lepervanche, M., 'Australian Immigrants, 1788-1940: Desired and Unwanted' in Wheelwright, E.L. & Buckley, K. (eds), *Essays in the Political Economy of Australian Capitalism*, Vol. 1, Sydney: ANZ Books, 1975.

Del Mastro, P.M., 'Italian Immigration to Australia 1920-1940: The Sammarchese', MA thesis, Monash University, 1986.

Dolin, J.E., 'The Timber Industry of Western Australia', MA thesis, University of Western Australia, 1967.

Gabbedy, J.P., *The Forgotten Pioneers*, Fremantle: Fremantle Arts Centre Press, 1981.

Gamba, C., 'The Italian Immigration to Western Australia', MA thesis, University of Western Australia, 1949.

Gentilli, J., *Italian Roots in Australian Soil. Italian Migration to Western Australia 1829-1946*, Perth: Italo-Australian Welfare Centre, 1983.

Gregory, J. (ed.), *On the Homefront: Western Australia and World War II*, Nedlands: University of Western Australia Press, 1996.

Hartley, A.E., 'The Organization of Timber Production in the Hardwood Forests of Western Australia', MA thesis, University of Western Australia, 1946.

Hill, P. M., *Macedonians in Australia*, Perth: Hesperian Press, 1989.

Jupp, J. (ed.), *The Australian People: An Encyclopaedia of the Nation, its People and their Origins*, Sydney: Angus & Robertson, 1988.

Langfield, M., '"White aliens": The control of European immigration to Australia 1920-30' in *Journal of Intercultural Studies*, Vol. 12 (2), 1991.

Lowenstein, W., & Loh, M., *The Immigrants*, Melbourne: (Pelican Books) Penguin, 1985.

Markus, A., 'Labour and Immigration: Policy Formulation 1943-45', *Labour History*, No. 46, May 1984.

- 'Labour and Immigration 1946-49: The Displaced Persons Program', *Labour History*, No. 47, November 1984.

Mills, J., *The Timber People*, Perth: Wescolour Press for Bunnings Ltd., 1986.

Owens, D., *Jardee: The Mill That Cheated Time*, UWA Press for the Charles and Joy Staples South West Region Publication Fund, 1994.

Price, C.A., *Southern Europeans in Australia*, Melbourne: Oxford University Press, 1963.

Robertson, J.R., 'History of the Timber Industry of Western Australia', *University Studies*, Vol. III No. 1, 1957, pp. 51-59.

Sambrailo, M.L., 'Dalmatian Croats in Western Australia 1870-1920', unpublished paper, 34pp.

- 'From a Rocky Coast to Sandy Shores: Dalmatian immigrants from the Goldfields to Spearwood 1920s - 1940s', unpublished paper, 24pp.

- 'Exodus to Egypt: Yugoslav Refugees Across Egypt to Australia: 1944-1947', unpublished paper, 22pp.
Snooks, G.D., *Depression and Recovery in Western Australia, 1928/29-1938/39*, Perth: University of Western Australia Press, 1974.
Splivalo, A., *The Home Fires*, Fremantle: Fremantle Arts Centre Press, 1982.
Strano, A., *Luck Without Joy: a portrayal of a migrant*, Fremantle: Fremantle Arts Centre Press, 1986.
Taylor, J.G., 'History of the timber industry in the South-west of WA', Busselton Historical Society Newsletter, September 1981, pp. 1-3.
Thompson, S.L., *Australia Through Italian Eyes*, Melbourne: Oxford University Press, 1980.
Tillman, J.A., *Donnelly Men and Mill*, Bunbury, W.A.:Excelsior Print, 1991.
Tkalcevic, M., *Croats in Australian Society*, Melbourne Government Press, 1980.
- Croats in Australia: An Information and Resource Guide, Melbourne: Victoria College Press, 1989.

About the Author

Christina grew up on the island of Malta. She travelled extensively with her husband Bjorn, living for short periods in Geneva, Stockholm and Iran before finally settling in Western Australia in 1982. Christina obtained a doctorate in social/political science at Murdoch University in 1998.

Christina's professional career included lecturing at West Australian Universities, management positions within the public service of WA, sitting on the bench of the Equal Opportunity Tribunal and public policy consultant to the Premier of WA. In 2008, she decided that it was time to realise a long held dream and go sailing around the world. After eleven years of sailing and travelling, Christina took up the pen again, this time branching out from academic writing into fiction and biography, apart from occasional work as a consultant to the European Union's Coastal Management projects. In 2018, she returned with her husband to live in Perth. They have two children, a son and a daughter, and three grandchildren.

Addendum

This book is based on my doctoral thesis entitled *From Aliens to Ethnics: Identity and Citizenship in a Study of Italians and Croatians in the Western Australian Southwest Timber Industry 1919-1969*, (Murdoch University, 1998). The thesis provides a more detailed account of this history with full referencing.

Dr Christina Gillgren

www.ingramcontent.com/pod-product-compliance
Lightning Source LLC
Chambersburg PA
CBHW051426290426
44109CB00016B/1453